SURFING

Newport Beach

THE GLORY DAYS OF CORONA DEL MAR

CLAUDINE E. BURNETT
& PAUL BURNETT

Charleston   London

THE
History
PRESS

Published by The History Press
Charleston, SC 29403
www.historypress.net

Photos courtesy of the Surfing Heritage & Culture Center, First American Title Insurance
Company's Historical Collection, Orange County Archives, Sherman Library, the authors
and "Woody" Woodworth.

First published 2013

Manufactured in the United States

ISBN 978.1.60949.840.5

Library of Congress CIP data applied for.

*Dedicated to the surfers who first rode
Corona del Mar/Newport Beach
and whose souls continue to ride the
spirit waves of Corona del Mar.*

Contents

Contents

Acknowledgements

Our thanks to all those who have helped us in our quest to keep Newport Beach history alive: the Sherman Library and Gardens, the Newport Beach Public Library, the Orange County Historical Society, the Surfing Heritage & Culture Center, the Newport Beach Historical Society, the Newport Harbor Nautical Museum, the Balboa Island Museum and Historical Society, First American Trust, Jill Thrasher, Spencer Croul, Steve Farwell, Sharon Marshall, "Woody" Woodworth, Nancy Gardner, Steve Cleary and Steve Wilkings.

We'd also like to thank the Vultee, Waters, Thomas, Zahn, Ball, Peterson, Gregg and Huffman families, whose photos, donated to the Surfing Heritage & Culture Center, are used in this book.

Introduction

Today, Newport Beach is considered the uncrowned jewel of Orange County's "Gold Coast," the glitz-and-glamour center of the West Coast. It's a city composed of various communities, including Corona del Mar, Balboa Island, Balboa Peninsula, Newport Coast, San Joaquin Hills, Santa Ana Heights and West Newport. Here there are multimillion-dollar residences, million-dollar yachts and usually two Mercedes and a Jaguar in garages the size of most people's homes. But the Newport Beach you're going to find in this book is quite different. It's the Newport Beach before World War II—a lively, lusty, beach resort where rum runners openly docked and unloaded their illegal brew and where drinking, gambling and dancing paid the bills. It was a city that was hell on wheels from Memorial Day to Labor Day before going into hibernation the rest of the year except for a brief awakening during Easter vacation. It was a city where every weekend during the summer there was some aquatic event that included wave riding—but not the kind you think of today. Aquaboarding was the "common man's" way of tackling the ocean, standing on an aquaplane board, holding on to an attached rope and being pulled by a boat—an early ancestor of water skiing.

Back then, surfboards were big and heavy. The most famous surfer of the age, Duke Kahanamoku, rode the waves of Newport Bay in a canoe, and when he could, he borrowed an actual surfboard from his friend Felix Modjeski, grandson of famous Polish actress Madame Helena Modjeska, who owned a nearby beach cottage. Eventually, Duke and some of his friends brought their own surfboards to Corona del Mar and left them at the Sparr

Surfing the Newport Harbor channel in the 1930s.

Bathhouse (the boards were too heavy to carry back and forth), starting what would become one of the first surf clubs in the United States—the Corona del Mar Surf Club. It was this club that initiated the first surf contest on the mainland—the Pacific Coast Surfboard Championship in 1928—but even then canoes were featured in the main events!

The surf changed as the bay changed. In the 1920s, an eight-hundred-foot cement jetty was constructed off the rocks at Corona del Mar. It was a bodysurfer's treat. You could get into a wave at the end of the jetty on the channel side, ride in next to the jetty for an eight-hundred-foot long adventure, climb up a chain ladder, run out on the jetty and do the same thing all over again all day long. Unfortunately, it was difficult for boaters to get through the channel due to sandbars and the waves. Alas, a new jetty, completed in 1936, destroyed the perpetual surf at Corona del Mar.

Surfing also changed with innovations to surfboard construction. With these newer, lighter boards, more people were drawn to Newport and Corona del Mar (across the bay from Newport) to enjoy the fabulous surf of the 1920s and '30s.

In later years, college students would be blamed for all of the headaches brought on by Bal Week in the 1960s and '70s. However, the young people were only carrying on a tradition that had begun in the late 1920s with the

Corona del Mar looking west, circa 1922.

opening of the Rendezvous Ballroom. Thousands of high school and college students poured into Newport Beach during their annual spring break. Huge parties and endless traffic jams were the norm on the peninsula during that one fun-filled week. The Rendezvous Ballroom first became home to the "big bands" of the 1930s, and then in the 1960s, it adopted Dick Dale, "King of the Surf Guitar."

It was in Newport Beach that the phenomena of Southern California surfing took on the persona it has today. That may be why so many surf manufacturers, including Quiksilver, Volcom and Hurley, made their homes here—they wanted to be close to the roots of their trade.

Chapter 1

The Bay

It's impossible to understand the surfing conditions around Newport Beach without a brief history of the Santa Ana River and Newport Bay. From the harbor entrance at the rocky headland at Corona del Mar, Newport Bay extends north-northeast about three and a half miles behind a narrow sandspit called the Balboa Peninsula. The bay actually combines two distinct bodies of water, "Upper" and "Lower" Newport Bay, with the Pacific Coast

Newport Bay before any breakwater.

Highway Bridge dividing the two sections. The Upper Bay is mainly an estuary, with fresh water flowing in from San Diego Creek, Big Canyon, local springs and drainage from nearby areas. The Lower Bay today includes five man-made islands—Linda, Harbor, Balboa, Lido and Bay Islands—but in the past there were no islands, and the Lower Bay was much different. There was a time when the Santa Ana River flowed directly into the Lower Bay and there were no jetties.

EARLY DAYS TO THE 1910S

Throughout its history, the Santa Ana River has frequently overflowed its banks and changed its main channel. At one time, it flowed through the present-day cities of Anaheim and Westminster, finally reaching the sea at Alamitos Bay. But it also established another route across a broad flood plain between the Newport and Huntington Beach mesas.

In the early days, before farming became the major industry of Orange County, there were no dams or levees controlling the Santa Ana River as it followed its course from the San Bernardino Mountains. At the end of its journey near Newport, it disappeared into peat beds covered with willows and tules, which created almost impenetrable thickets. This area served as a sieve, catching the silt and sand carried by the river from upland areas and creating a lagoon. Gradually, an offshore barrier beach formed, growing down the coast until it enclosed the lagoon that is now Lower Newport Bay. The river, imprisoned behind the sandspit, turned down the coast through the lagoon and out to sea.

Many believe that this barrier beach was permanently breached during the floods of 1824–25, which brought additional silt into the bay, creating Balboa Peninsula and the sandbars that would later become Balboa, Lido, Bay, Harbor and Linda Islands. H.L. Sherman, in his *History of Newport Beach*, hypothesized that the sandspit that would eventually become Balboa Peninsula grew all the way from the Huntington Beach mesa to an area opposite the east end of Lido Isle in a period of about thirty-three years, from 1825 to 1858. He also theorized that the sandspit had its last spurt of growth, from the end of Lido Isle almost to Corona del Mar, in the single flood season of 1861–62.

Though Sherman's theory is disputed by some, we do have a report by the United States Coast Survey, published in 1861, which had this to say about the bay:

The lagoon was found to be some five miles long and separated from the ocean by a narrow strip of sand-beach, over which the heavy southeast and northwest swells was in every gale. The outlet or mouth is 50 yards in width, with a narrow bar outside. Over this bar there is a frightful swell rolling and tumbling at all stages of the tide, making it dangerous to cross in boats of any kind.

Early settlers transformed the swampy area surrounding the river. They drained the area, removed trees and planted crops, but farmers complained about the periodic overflowing of the river. In May 1907, the owners of seventeen thousand acres of some of the richest soil in Orange County organized to prevent future flooding of the Santa Ana River. They voted to form a district extending from Newport and the west edge of Santa Ana to beyond Talbert (present-day Fountain Valley). Combining the names Newport and Talbert, the new district was called the Newbert Protection District. Later that same year, Newbert Protection District officials were successful in passing a $185,000 bond to build levees and a three-hundred-foot-wide channel, the channel leading directly into the west end of Lower Newport Bay through a right-of-way also secured with the bond. Part of this channel is still visible today, between Cappy's

The 1907 channel that originally led directly into Newport Bay is still visible today.

15

The Newport bluff above the original 1907 Santa Ana River channel that led directly to the bay.

Café (5930 West Coast Highway) and the end of the bluffs next to Pacific Coast Highway.

But by 1912, the newly channeled river had already carried considerable silt into the lower bay. Heavy rains in March 1914 choked the channel at the point where it met Newport Bay tidewater with not only silt but also tree stumps, dead animals and other types of debris. So massive was the debris that not even the tides could move in or out. Shellfish smothered, and it took days to unclog the filled channels. Fortunately, the channel was clear enough for famed surfer/swimmer Duke Kahanamoku to ride the breakers at the harbor entrance in September 1914, but later that same year, one of the most destructive storms of the century hit the region. In December 1914, water in the bay rose eight inches above the high-tide mark, ocean waves undermined peninsula houses and gas and water mains were destroyed. Within five months, another flood brought more destruction, and the Santa Ana River was deemed the worst flood threat west of the Mississippi by the Army Corps of Engineers.

In June 1915, as a result of these regional floods, the California Legislature enacted a law allowing cities and counties to bond themselves for reclamation projects. On September 25, 1916, the citizens of Newport Beach voted

One of the many early farms in Orange County in the Santa Ana River floodplain.

$125,000 to build one jetty off the Balboa Peninsula. As Americans went off to fight in World War I, Newport Beach began construction. In September 1917, with the war in Europe still raging, five thousand people celebrated as the first jetty rock was dropped in place. Temporarily forgetting the world's troubles, a celebration was held that included yacht racing, canoe tilting and surfboard riding.

Aspirations of becoming a United States naval base led Newport politicians to ask for another election to allocate funds for improving the bay. It had also become apparent that the Santa Ana River was not happy with its 1907 channel and levees. During heavy rains and flooding in January 1916, the river hammered its way through the sand until it decided to cut itself a new path to the ocean nearly due east of Huntington Beach. By January 21, 1916, it was flowing smoothly through a brand-new channel, almost directly west and with its new outlet to the ocean nearly five miles above the old. By May 1916, the break in the levee was fixed, but it was apparent that the channel allowing the Santa Ana River direct access to Newport Bay was not working. Inflowing tides were encroaching upon hundreds of acres of rich farmland.

In 1919, it was decided that funds were needed to dredge a channel along the inner shore of the Balboa Peninsula, lengthen the new Peninsula jetty

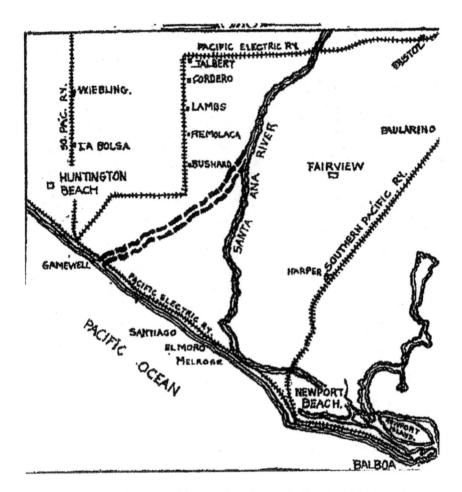

This 1916 map shows the course of the new channel carved by flooding of the Santa Ana River. The old channel lay at the base of the hills in the background and emptied into Newport Bay, about five miles south. On this map, the new course is shown by the dotted lines.

(also known as the West jetty) and divert the Santa Ana River from entering the bay. In June 1919, a $500,000 bond was approved to divert the Santa Ana River from Newport Bay, lengthen the Peninsula jetty two hundred feet and build it up to a depth of twenty-two feet and dredge a sixteen-foot-deep three-mile channel inside the bay.

THE 1920s

By December 1920, a new outlet for the Santa Ana River had been cut directly to the sea between Newport Beach and Huntington Beach, and rock jetties were built to keep the outlet open. An earthen dam, twelve feet high, sixty feet wide at the base and fifteen feet wide at the top, had also been constructed across the river's old channel at Bitter Point.

By early 1921, the Peninsula jetty extension was finished, making the structure 1,900 feet long. Early resident Robert Gardner didn't think much of the jetty. In his book *Bawdy Balboa*, Gardner described it as being too short and sagging down at the surf line until the rocks were underwater. In other words, at the most important part, it was practically no jetty at all.

If you go down to the seashore and stand in shallow water, letting the waves wash back and forth around your feet, you will feel the scouring effect that sunk the jetty rocks closest to shore. You will find that you slowly sink into the sand until your feet and ankles are totally covered. This happens because you have only the sand to act as a foundation under you. The same

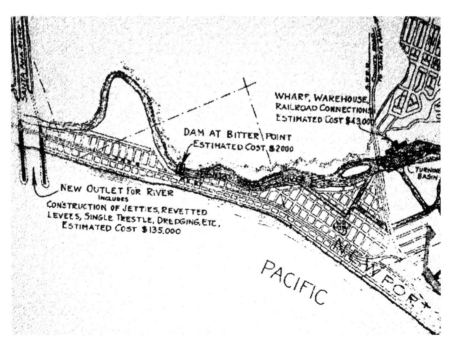

This map shows plans for the 1919–21 Newport Harbor work. Today, drivers can detect a slight rise and fall on Pacific Coast Highway between Cappy's Café (5930 West Coast Highway) and the spot where the bluffs turn inland. This marks the old exit of the Santa Ana River into the bay and the base of the Bitter Point Dam.

If you follow the water channel next to Cappy's Café until it reaches the Santa Ana River, you are actually going along the old riverbed, which existed before the Bitter Point Dam was built and the river diversion was completed.

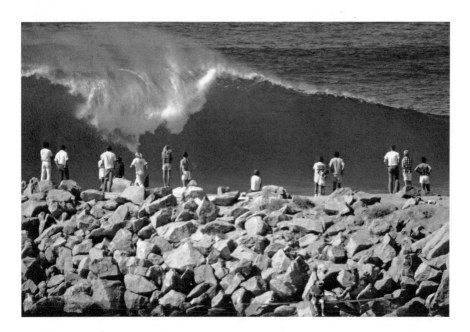

The Wedge today, breaking west of the Peninsula jetty.

thing happened to the jetty. Without a firm foundation, the part of the jetty closest to shore simply sank, letting the waves and currents go right on through it. This slow sinking was to give gradual birth to the Newport Beach surfing landmark known as the "Wedge."

The sinking of the jetty rocks closest to shore did not ring any alarm bells at the time, except for the builders, who realized they had miscalculated. However, what the ocean was attempting to do was build the Wedge, and the ocean only stopped because the rocks sank.

With the completion of the last Peninsula jetty in 1936, the Wedge fully emerged, demonstrating its full strength when conditions were just right. The large waves the Wedge is known for are produced when a wave (usually a south swell) approaches the shore at the proper angle and reflects off the jetty, creating a second wave. The reflected wave then meets up with the following wave of the set and forms a peak. This pattern can repeat for several following waves as well. The combined effect of the reflected wave and the incoming wave creates a combined wave much larger than either of the two separate waves. This occurs very quickly, forming waves in an unpredictable and unstable pattern, so that no two waves are alike and the exact breaking point is difficult to predict. The combination of very large, irregular waves breaking in extremely shallow water, along with the constant hazard of encountering backwash, is the reason riders are drawn to what Bruce Brown in his film *Endless Summer* calls the "Dirty Old Wedge."

In 1922, surfing legend Duke Kahanamoku again visited Newport Beach to see if surf conditions had changed since the addition of the Peninsula jetty. (According to fellow surfers Tom Blake and Art Vultee, Kahanamoku had surfed here back in 1912, either on his way to the Olympics or on his return journey. Although this cannot be independently confirmed, he did come back again in 1914 amid much acclaim from the local press.) "The Duke," as he was affectionately referred to, expressed delight at the ideal surfing conditions created by the sandbars, which caused big breakers to roll in for a long distance. But in reality, the surf often broke all the way across the channel mouth. It made taking a boat in or out of the bay a chancy undertaking. On an average day, it was tricky—on a big day, suicide. It was good for surfing but not for boats.

By 1923, the flaws of the Peninsula jetty were openly acknowledged. It looked like all the money spent on improving Lower Newport Bay hadn't been enough. The one jetty was neither high enough nor long enough. The sandbar in the entrance was getting bigger, and channels dredged inside

The surf often broke all the way across the Newport channel mouth before 1936. It was good for surfing but not for boats.

the bay had become shallow. Even the rum runners who openly docked in Balboa were having a hard time getting their cargo through. In June 1924, the sandbars in the bay forced a gang smuggling their illegal booze ashore to unload cargo at Irvine Cove, five miles south of Balboa. Customs agents from Los Angeles arrested them and confiscated their liquor, valued at $12,000. Also seized were three automobiles worth $11,000.

The Balboa Peninsula was divided into three communities known as Newport, East Newport and Balboa. The fledgling village of Corona del Mar was across the bay. It was in Balboa where all the action took place and rum runners had free reign. Balboa resident Robert Gardner remembered that a stream of big, black sedans would line up on the peninsula around midnight on evenings when the tide was right. As the drivers stood around smoking cigarettes, the rumbling roar of high-speed motorboats could be heard in the bay bringing the illicit freight to the city dock. It was all very open. There was nothing furtive about it, except when federal agents paid an unexpected visit to town, which is what happened on December 31, 1924, when one rum runner was reportedly killed, a $50,000 cargo of imported liquor was captured and a $10,000 yacht and two automobiles were seized. It was an episode that locals talked about for years.

Perhaps it was the complaints of these rum runners that got Newport Beach residents to do something about the treacherous sandbars. But the "official" story involves an amazing rescue by none other than Duke Kahanamoku.

Many lives would have been lost aboard the *Thelma* if Duke Kahanamoku hadn't been in Corona del Mar on the morning of June 14, 1925, to rescue its occupants when the boat capsized. Years before, Duke and several friends had discovered the long sandbar that reached out into the ocean from the Corona del Mar main beach, along with the beautiful surf that built up on that sandbar. They began leaving their surfboards at the Sparr Bathhouse (also known as the Corona del Mar Bathhouse), returning when they could to enjoy the surf. That June morning, seventeen men were thrown into the churning water from the *Thelma*. Witnessing the tragedy, Kahanamoku pounded into the surf with his surfboard, rescuing seven victims in three trips. Others took to their boards and rescued five more, but sadly, five men drowned. This heroic work was the first convincing demonstration of the usefulness of the surfboard in life saving. It also convinced Newport Beach residents that something had to be done about the sandbars accumulating at the mouth of the harbor entrance.

In February 1927, voters endorsed a $500,000 bond to construct a concrete east jetty off Corona del Mar and an extension of the original

Corona del Mar looking west, circa 1927.

The concrete Corona del Mar jetty and the Peninsula jetty across the harbor entrance.

peninsula one, but the work was poorly planned. Voters thought they were endorsing a project that would be implemented under the direction of the Army Corps of Engineers, but instead it was being drawn up by the Newport Beach city engineer.

General Lansing Beach, former chief of engineers of the United States Army, had publicly declared that Newport Beach belonged to a small, exclusive list of Pacific Coast cities that could reasonably expect to have harbors. According to Beach, it was one of only three natural harbors between San Diego and San Francisco Bays and was the best of the three. Acting upon Beach's laudatory remarks, voters approved funding for harbor improvements. But it was Paul Kressley, Newport Beach city engineer, working on a commission basis, who got the job.

One of Kressley's biggest mistakes was designing and constructing a jetty on the Corona del Mar side of the bay (also known as the East jetty) of reinforced concrete instead of rock. On the peninsula, the construction crew, under Kressley's directions, simply extended the Pacific Electric rail line from Main Street down to the end of the point and then built a railway on pilings out over the Peninsula (West) jetty. They then sent flatcars loaded with rocks out on the Peninsula jetty and simply pushed the rocks off the flat cars. It wasn't very scientific, and it made a sloppy looking jetty. But their biggest

24

A surfer enjoys the wave break at the harbor mouth. The rail line used to build the 1927 Peninsula jetty extension can also be seen in the background.

mistake was putting a groin at the water's edge and curving that groin up toward Balboa a couple of hundred yards. It was a terrible decision. The groin caused a current to run up the coast toward Balboa and triggered erosion along the peninsula beach, undermining oceanfront homes and coming close to making another entrance to the bay at about M Street.

While the groin was at the water's edge, the kids loved it. Since it ran parallel to the ocean's edge, the surf broke right on the groin, not on the beach as it does now. Youngsters concocted a dangerous game of grabbing a big rock at the brink of the ocean and hanging on as the surf hit them. If the surf broke them loose from their rock, they lost. Today, if you go down to what is now called the Wedge and walk out toward the Peninsula jetty, look to your right and you will see the tops of some rocks making a little line up the beach toward the houses. That's how far away from the present shoreline the groin is now. It's still all there, but it's almost completely buried. It was also during this 1927 jetty extension that the Wedge fully emerged, its waves the byproduct of so-called improvements to the Peninsula jetty, which in actuality created the erosion along the peninsula beach.

Much to the dismay of boaters, the Newport Bay sandbar continued to grow, adding to the surf. The Corona del Mar concrete jetty was dubbed by locals as the "concrete wave-making machine." Both sides of the jetty

This shows the groin running up the peninsula from the jetty, where youngsters used to grab onto the rocks and play "Chicken." Also note the huge sandbar at the mouth of the bay.

These rises, barely visible in the sand, mark the 1927 groin of the Peninsula jetty.

Note the rocks to the left of the tree coming toward us—this is what's left of the 1927 groin of the Peninsula jetty.

were perpendicular or straight-sided and smooth. It made big waves out of little waves and monsters out of big ones. As the surf hit the end of the jetty, it would curl off on the channel side in a fantastic shape. The few board surfers stayed off the end and took shoulders either to the right or left. If a surfer couldn't catch the wave next to the Corona jetty, their friends would throw them a rope and pull them on their redwood board along the jetty. They would "pull 'em right into the wave," recalled longtime surfer Lorrin "Whitey" Harrison. With the jetty covered in marine slime, how the runner could do this and not end up falling and sliding remains a mystery.

The bodysurfers worked next to the Corona jetty. The waves would roll along the jetty, holding a perpetual shoulder—all you could ride in those pre–swim fin days. It was heaven on earth to bodysurfers, who got an eight-hundred-foot ride (the length of the Corona jetty) and then merely had to climb up a chain ladder, run back out on the jetty, dive in and do the same thing all over again.

The twelve-foot flat top of the concrete jetty was constantly covered with water—a perfect spot for the cultivation of marine moss. It was so slimy that it was almost impossible to walk on without slipping. This slick surface gave rise to another game among surfers almost as crazy as hanging onto a rock

A crowded day at the Corona jetty, 1930s.

A wave breaking along the Corona del Mar jetty.

Big Wave Day at the Corona del Mar jetty, circa 1930.

at the groin. Kids would run toward each other on the top of the jetty, throw themselves down on their bellies on this slick moss and slide toward each other, heads down. The goal of the game was to find out who would chicken out first. Sometimes neither turned chicken, in which case two careening bodies hit head to head. It was dumb…but fun.

For boaters, however, the faulty work on the jetties was humiliating and demoralizing to a resort city that had expected the summer of 1928 to be the greatest in its history. The Transpacific Yacht Race to Honolulu was scheduled to leave from the harbor entrance

The 1928 **Transpacific Yacht Race** from Newport Bay to Honolulu was won by Commodore Clem Stose, who claimed he went without sleep for sixteen days. The veteran San Diego yachtsman had sailed the 2,300 miles with an entirely green crew. Facing baffling calms, it wasn't until the sixth day from Newport Beach that he was able to strike northeast trade winds, which carried him to Honolulu aboard his yacht the *Teva*.

Walton Hubbard Jr. of the Newport Harbor Yacht Club had won the **International Star race** the previous year, but he was not to take home the coveted trophy again. After five days of racing off the Southern California coast, it was H.E. Edrington Jr. of New Orleans who won the 1928 championship by one point and one-twelfth of a boat length.

at the end of May. The opening of Lido Isle was planned for July 8, and the International Star races were scheduled for August, the first time they had ever been held on the West Coast. How could these races be held when the depth of the water over the sandbar in the entrance was only four feet at low tide? To meet this emergency, a committee was formed. The committee raised $10,000 from private donations, including pennies from school children, to hire a small dredger to perform $10,000 worth of dredging. Fortunately, work was completed in time for Memorial Day and the beginning of the Transpacific Yacht Race. In August, to highlight the International Star yacht races, a huge celebration was held. Part of the festivities included the first Pacific Coast Surfboard Competition, hosted by the Corona del Mar Surf Club.

1930-1941

Harbor and beach improvements were also being carried out by the West Newport Improvement Association. The group had succeeded in launching a dredging program that resulted in much of the swampy land in the area of West Newport being filled in and deeper channels made where boats could travel. It also petitioned the city to dredge the old canals that had been filled with silt and sand in the floods of 1914–16, and with this dredging it was able to build up Newport Island (off Balboa Boulevard and Thirty-eighth Street) to a height of eleven feet above high tide. Its last objective was the installation of groins along the oceanfront near Thirty-sixth Street to help build up the beach. The frivolous, fun days of the 1920s ended with the stock market crash in October 1929, though it took some time for folks to realize it.

In 1930, the Newport Harbor Chamber of Commerce reported that building for eleven months of 1930 was $164,105 greater than for all twelve months of 1929, which was $117,685 greater than 1928. In addition, the Newport Packing Company had taken over the old Newport cannery, built in 1919, with hopes of revitalizing the fish-packing plant.

All in all, the Great Depression did have a positive effect on Newport Beach. The Federal Public Works Administration agreed to allocate funding to help revitalize the bay if Orange County citizens consented to pay $640,000 of the $1,830,000 project. In December 1933, Orange County voters OK'd the additional county funding for harbor improvements. Now 322,000 tons of rock would be deposited on both the Corona (East) and Peninsula (West) jetties, making each 2,800 feet in length. In addition, dredging would add extra sand

Enjoying the surf and the jetty at Corona del Mar.

to Newport Island, create Linda Isle and extend the beaches next to both the Corona and Peninsula jetties. The completed Newport Harbor, with its long jetties, deep channels, anchorages and newly widened peninsula beach, was dedicated on May 23, 1936. It ruined Corona del Mar as a "surfing machine," although it did improve the safety in the channel mouth for boaters.

The designers of the Corona side jetty add-on did all they could to make sure the "surfing machine" would never come back to life. First, they changed the direction of the new jetty add-on so that it ran a few degrees more to the west than the old jetty. Second, they added a finger jetty at the end of the concrete jetty at a right angle to it and into the harbor channel about fifty feet. Finally, they dropped boulders next to the old concrete jetty all along the channel side and along about one third of the Corona side.

Intrepid surfers didn't let the dredging stop them from enjoying the waves. As the dredging was going on, surfers such as Whitey Harrison kept surfing in the channel. Harrison recalled cables running across the surf break and out to the dredge. "We'd be riding, and we'd have to jump the cable or lay down on our back to go under it," recalled Harrison. "We thought it was great fun to go out there with the construction going on, surfing in all that."

But the Santa Ana River still persisted in claiming Newport Bay. The usually quiet river could become destructive, which is what it did once again in March 1938, when over two hundred people throughout the Southland lost their lives because of the disastrous flood and rainstorm. Over one hundred bridges were washed out, and there were more than 150 landslides. Many towns, such as Anaheim and Fullerton, were under water. The river broke from its banks in five places, flooding thirty thousand acres to a depth of five feet or more and leaving two thousand homeless.

The 1938 weather disaster, the worst to hit the region during the twentieth century, led to the building of the Prado Dam in 1941. The ninety-mile Santa Ana River waterway, which begins in the San Bernardino Mountains near Big Bear, empties into the sea at the northern tip of Newport Beach. The devastation wouldn't have happened if, in 1929, voters had approved a bond measure to build a dam near Weir Canyon. They had forgotten the flood of 1916, which killed four people and damaged cropland. Instead, they were still focused on recovering from the costly 6.3-magnitude earthquake that had been centered off Newport in March 1933. But money was very tight, and the inevitable happened. For five days beginning February 27, 1938, at least twenty-two inches of rain fell in the mountains, most of it flowing into the Santa Ana River. By 2:00 a.m. on March 3, the river was moving at 100,000 cubic feet per second, and it soon breached its levees. Newspapers reported runoff from local mountains that were so severe the Santa Ana River's chocolate-colored water spread like a fan across western Orange County, creating a lake out of much of the lowlands. The floodwaters twisted railroad tracks, washed parts of Pacific Coast Highway out into the sea and carried entire houses down streets and through orange groves.

It might have been a surfer's dream when fifteen-foot waves crested in the Santa Ana River during the flood of 1938, but it was a nightmare to others when bridges collapsed, sending chunks of concrete flying through the air. Years later, in January 1969, when accumulated floodwaters were released from the Prado Dam, surfers were seen riding their boards on several of the flood control channels and even in the streets of Orange, where water flowed curb-high in some areas!

While the area was still rebuilding from this tragedy, another calamity hit—the Hurricane of 1939. "Strange weather" was the phrase that local residents used to describe the events of September 1939. After a record-breaking heat wave during which thermometers soared to 119 degrees in Orange, a storm ravaged the Newport Beach coast. When the storm was over, at least forty-five people were dead, most of them boaters who made the fatal mistake of trying to come ashore in thundering surf. Sixty had already died of heat prostrations in the seven days preceding the horrific storm.

Heavy ocean swells began to pound the Southern California coast on Saturday afternoon, September 23, 1939. If this had been the East Coast, it would have meant only one thing: the onset of a tropical storm. Small boats would have headed for a safe refuge, and ships would have stood out to sea, but this was California, and things like that didn't happen here. On September 24, gray overcast skies moved in, and winds moved up rapidly from Force 1 to Force 11, hurricane level.

Many of the two thousand boats in Newport Harbor were already at sea, some having taken off that Friday for Catalina Island. Newport's dory fleet was at sea when suddenly—and without warning—the boats were in trouble. Some chose to ride the storm out in the open water, but dozens immediately headed for Newport Harbor and what they thought would be safety. Instead, they discovered a harbor mouth with two rock jetties waiting to devour them between rows of stone teeth. Many shot the gap between the jetties successfully, but about a dozen didn't make it. The cresting waves at the mouth of the harbor lifted propellers and rudders out of the water, and out-of-control boats slammed into the rocks, breaking apart on impact.

Many more lives would have been lost if it wasn't for two fearless surfers. The *Jolly Tom*, a thirty-three-foot cruiser, hit the rocks and disintegrated, leaving five adults and four children clinging to whatever wreckage they could find. Nineteen-year-old John Lugo and his friend Ralph Dawson had just returned from a day of surfing at San Onofre, where the surf was big and consistent, the water warm and the sun very hot. When the storm hit San Onofre, everyone left. John and Ralph stopped at Corona del Mar to watch the storm from the cliffs above the beach. Huge surf was breaking all the way across the entrance between the new jetties and rolling along with about ten feet of white water quite a distance into the bay. They saw the *Jolly Tom* hit the rocks. Without even thinking, the boys jumped into the water and spent the next hour paddling the survivors to safety on their surfboards. Lugo was a well-known Newport Beach lad whose father was a local plumber. In July 1929, John had made headline news in the *Balboa Times* by selling the most newspaper subscriptions (103,450). Now he made the news again by paddling to the overturned boat and saving the people trapped in the cabin.

Heavy surf at Corona del Mar. In 1939, surfers John Lugo and
Ralph Dawson saved the lives of nine boaters by paddling through
massive surf to rescue them.

During the storm, between four and five inches of rain fell, causing
massive flooding. Newport was the first area hit by the hurricane. Suffering
major damage was the Balboa Peninsula, where violent surf along with
debris from wrecked piers and barges pounded homes built along the sand.
Piers up and down the coast were heavily damaged. Most of the Balboa Pier
and a four-hundred-foot section of the Newport Pier were smashed, as was
Seal Beach landing and a number of homes in the Sunset Beach area.

Chapter 2

Newport Beach Before Surfing

NATIVE AMERICANS, THE SPANISH AND FARMERS

We've already given you a glimpse of Newport Beach before surfing in our narrative on Newport Bay. However, we must not forget Native Americans from the village of Geng-na, on the mesa above the bay, who were the first paddleboarders to navigate the Newport inlet and to tackle the surf off Newport. From their seasonal campsite, which now lies beneath the streets of Corona del Mar, they built canoes, tying bundles of tules together and caulking them with asphalt picked up along the beach. Like the native Hawaiians who would invent the sport of surfing, these Newport natives ventured far afield, traveling to the offshore islands of Catalina and San Clemente in pursuit of trade. But as you've already read, Newport Bay was quite different then, as the Santa Ana River changed its course many times.

In 1542, Spanish sailor and explorer Juan Rodriguez Cabrillo sailed into the Newport area, calling the beautiful bay that he found Bay de las Fumas de Temblores. Off of a sandspit that would later become the Balboa Peninsula, he was to find deep-water approaches closer to the shoreline than at any other point on the Southern California coast. Just 2,500 feet offshore, the depth was ten fathoms. This deep-water approach would become important in 1888, when a wharf, the first of many, was built by James McFadden at the site of the present-day Newport Pier.

In 1864, the Newport Bay rancho holdings of Jose Sepulveda were sold to Flint, Bixby & Company and James Irvine. In 1876, James Irvine would buy out

Newport Landing, at present-day Coast Highway and Dover Drive, served as Orange County's shipping port from 1870 to 1889.

As far back as 1882, the large waves that often strike the Newport inlet made news. On March 13, 1882, the Firebaugh family was standing at their door watching the rain when a peculiar noise drew their attention to Newport Bay. To their horror, they noticed a large wave of water, accompanied by a heavy wind, crossing the mesa above Newport. The wind accompanying the wave blew over a neighbor's corncrib and haystack and whirled a cow that was tied nearby around like a top. It next struck the Henry Bush house, moving it about ten inches. (*Los Angeles Times*, March 16, 1882.)

his partners, making Newport his own. It wasn't until 1870, however, that the bay acquired the name of Newport. The name was the result of the hope that the bay once known as Bolsa de San Joann would become the "new port" for the region.

It all came about when a little steamer named *Vaquero* ventured through the treacherous sandbar at the mouth of the bay to unload goods from San Diego. The ship should have disposed of her cargo at Anaheim Landing (near present-day Seal Beach), but it owed so much money there that it decided to try another approach instead. All agreed that the arrival of the *Vaquero* signaled the beginning of a "new port." To encourage further commerce, James Irvine and the McFadden brothers, James and Robert, built a warehouse and wharf at the present intersection of Pacific Coast Highway and Dover Drive. They called it Newport Landing.

A City Begins

The sleepy seaside town that would be known as Newport Beach was open to the outside world in 1891 when a steam railroad was put through from Santa Ana. Life was different before the arrival of the railroad, as the August 3, 1883 issue of the *Los Angeles Times* indicates:

> *A Few Things that Newport Can Crow Over*
>
> - *That we have raised the most corn to the acre of any other locality in the county.*
> - *That we have raised the largest beet that was ever raised in the county, weight, 230 pounds; raised on the Wakeham farm by Mr. Welsh.*
> - *That we raise and export more fat hogs than any one shipping point in the valley.*
> - *That we have the best resort for pleasure seekers in the county.*
> - *That we have the advantage over any other place for shipping our produce, either from Newport Harbor or Santa Ana depot.*
> - *That we will soon have a No. 1 pork-packing house; also, a large cheese factory which is in progress.*

Most agree that development of Newport Beach really began in 1892. That was the year in which James McFadden purchased the major part of the Balboa Peninsula (from Fortieth Street to Ninth Street) for a dollar an acre; laid out a town site near the wharf, which he called Newport; and began to sell land. With money from this venture he was able, in 1896, to buy more marshland, which he filled in to create Balboa, Lido and Harbor islands. An article from the January 1, 1898 *Los Angeles Times* describes the scene:

> *The most noted and popular resort of Orange County is Newport. This has long been a favorite camping ground for residents of the inland part of Orange County. It is only during the past few years that it has come into prominence,*

McFadden's Wharf, site of the present-day Newport Pier, December 1892.

especially since it has been connected with Santa Ana by rail. There is a wharf over 1,200 feet long, ample hotel accommodations, a number of cottages to rent, also tents, besides which a number of citizens have private cottages. Provisions are brought to the doors of visitors. There is good water, and telephone connections are made with the town. Excellent bathing may be enjoyed; there is boating on the bay, clams are plentiful and the fishing from the wharf is excellent, the variety of fish caught being very great.

The nationwide economic depression of the 1890s coupled with the transfer of the railroad and wharf to millionaire J. Ross Clark (who owned the Los Alamitos sugar beet factory and the railroad that would eventually become the Southern Pacific) in 1899 led to a decline in the maritime shipping business that had kept Newport alive. Clark used the railroad and pier for his own business ventures, with little interest in accommodating other shipping concerns. Despite all the accolades given the town by the *Los Angeles Times*, by the turn of the twentieth century, Newport was nearly deserted. James McFadden decided it was time to sell, and in 1902, he sold the town site of Newport to developer William S. Collins.

Collins took on Henry E. Huntington as partner in his new Newport Beach Company in exchange for $37,000 and a promise to bring the Pacific

Electric to Newport. Collins gave Huntington's Pacific Electric one hundred feet of right-of-way along the Newport sandspit (later known as Balboa Peninsula) and the mudflat that was to become Lido Island. It was a good exchange, though racked with some political maneuverings.

What was this new development like? An article from the July 4, 1902 *Los Angeles Times* tells us:

NEWPORT BEACH NEVER SO OVERUN BEFORE

At least 8,000 people visited Newport Beach today, which is the largest crowd this seaside town has ever seen. Almost everyone from Santa Ana headed for the beach, and there were a good many people from other Southern California cities as well. The crowd enjoyed the patriotic day. The town was well decorated, and there was a free clambake.

Hundreds of tourists took trains from Riverside and Los Angeles to Santa Ana, the jumping-off point to catch the rail line to Newport. Two thousand people waited at Santa Ana for the train to the beach. Only a small number could be squeezed into the coaches, and other cars had to be added to the line. The bathhouses were so overrun that they weren't able to handle the crowd that wanted to change their clothing to swim.

Patriotic speeches were given in the afternoon. They were followed by a display of water sports at the end of the wharf. The program ended with a realistic naval battle and the blowing up of a miniature battleship. Tonight there will be a splendid fireworks display ending with a very credible representation of the eruption of Mount Pelée.

The year 1905 was an important one for Newport Beach and for the sport of surfing. In Hawaii, native Hawaiians began the informal Hui Nalu (Club of the Waves), revitalizing native Hawaiian interest in the sport, an interest now free to develop with the waning of missionary influence over the islands. In Newport, the arrival of the Pacific Electric rail line on August 3, 1905, changed the city forever.

But the "Red Car line," as it came to be called, stopped short. Promoters of Balboa (at the end of the peninsula between Main and Ninth Streets) had to ante big to get into the game. Finally, on July 4, 1906, the Pacific Electric reached Balboa. Tourist draws were the newly completed $15,000 Balboa Pavilion and, on the ocean side opposite the Pavilion, the $8,000 Balboa Pier. However, despite a $10,000 bulkhead on the oceanfront, it seemed the pier designers didn't understand the current, and at very high tides, it was

The Balboa Pavilion became one of the city's first landmarks.

Today, when most people think of Balboa, they think of Balboa Island, across the bay. But the Balboa of this book was its own creature. Unlike the town site of Newport, which supported a fishing industry, Balboa survived on the gambling and tourist trade, later becoming known as the "Sin City" of Orange County. It would eventually join up with Newport (which had incorporated under the name of Newport Beach in 1906) and become part of Newport Beach in 1916.

impossible for boats to dock at the pier. This was remedied in January 1908, when the 600-foot pier was lengthened 216 feet.

The coming of the electric line meant that travelers were arriving every hour rather than twice a day, as with the steam rail line. Real estate sales skyrocketed, and the community began its transition to a choice residential district and major tourist town. Soon, an election for incorporation passed by a vote of 42-12. The first meeting of the new board of trustees was held on September 3, 1906. The City of Newport Beach was officially born. Farther down the peninsula, the community of Balboa was taking shape.

While Jack London was writing about the Hawaiian sport of surfing, Newport was deciding on its future, as described in the July 19, 1907 *Los Angeles Times*:

PORT ORANGE PLANS

Port Orange is the most recent development upon the shores of Newport Bay which promises improvement. Port Orange is situated upon the high bluffs at the head of the lower bay and is a magnificent site not only for homes but also for business enterprises which will follow in time the development of the bay as a harbor for deep-sea going vessels.

The land surrounding the bay is, and has been, controlled by James Irvine and his father for many years, having been obtained by the Irvine family through a Spanish grant years ago. It is claimed that this harbor is the logical shipping point for a vast area of the Southwest; that between 150,000 and 250,000 people will be served through it. That by the new electric railways it will be nearer the city of Los Angeles than the present port now is. That it offers a safer refuge for vessels, coming either up or going down the coast, than any harbor between San Diego and San Francisco.

It is the proposal of the Port Orange Company to start the wheels a going, which will, it is expected, make of Newport Bay a commercial center from a shipping point. With this idea in view, it is proceeding with extensive improvements upon its great tract of land lying along the bay, and the officers of the company assert they will spend half a million dollars in this work.

The site selected for the city of Port Orange and for the business section of the same is ideal. Under the bluffs and stretching into the bay is a great tract of low ground, yet well above high tide, where it is proposed to build slips for ships, warehouses, piers and all the other makings of a great harbor.

At present, a force of men is at work upon the uplands, and grading outfits, pipe-layers and other workmen are transforming the mesa into a townsite as fast as they can. From this site, where the cool breezes from the ocean blow the livelong day, is commanded a magnificent view of the ocean and bay.

Port Orange was not to become a major commercial harbor. When the United States took over control of the Panama Canal project in 1904, business interests on the West Coast smelled money. The building of the Panama Canal foretold wealth for commercial seaports on the California

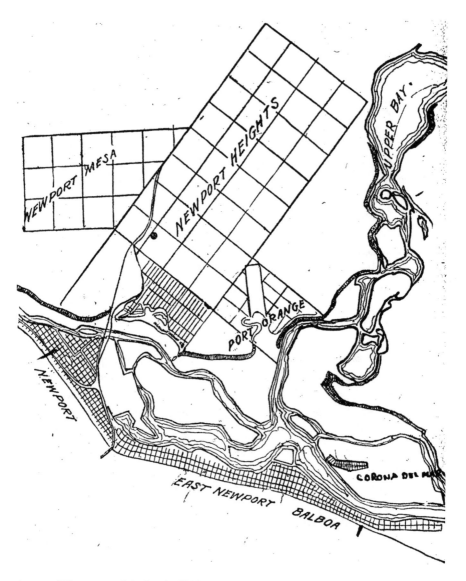

A map of Newport and the bay in 1907.

coast, and Southern California beach towns wanted in on the action, including Newport Beach. Cities along Santa Monica, Anaheim, Alamitos and San Pedro Bays were also in the running, with San Pedro Bay eventually becoming the winner.

Chapter 3

Surfing Arrives

THE 1900S AND 1910S

In 1907, California author Jack London visited Hawaii and discovered men who "walked on water," the phrase used to describe early surfing. It was eccentric journalist and wanderer Alexander Hume Ford who introduced London to Waikiki beach boy George Freeth. London was impressed by Freeth and his use of a surfboard. It must be remembered that in this time of heavy woolen bathing suits, the only aquatic "sport" available to California beachgoers was swimming. There were no surfboards, bodyboards or paddleboards to be seen off the California shore, just an occasional canoe drifting along with the ocean current. Someone who "walked on water" was indeed an amazing sight to those who lived at the beginning of the twentieth century!

According to a 1912 *Los Angeles Times* article, it was in 1900 that George Freeth revived the art of riding a surfboard in a standing position. Up to that time, Hawaiians rode their boards by lying on their stomachs, although they knew their early ancestors had ridden in a standing position. Freeth persisted in trying to ride the breakers erect but finally realized that the board he was using—sixteen feet long, four inches thick—couldn't take the curve in the combers. He finally worked out the proper dimensions—eight feet long, twenty-four inches wide and four inches thick. This design was quickly adopted by many Hawaiians who preferred to ride their surfboards standing up.

George Freeth brought the Hawaiian sport of surfing to California. He may have surfed Newport as early as 1907.

Jack London was amazed at what he saw, subsequently writing "Learning Hawaiian Surfing: A Royal Sport at Waikiki Beach, Honolulu" for the October 1907 issue of the *Ladies Home Companion*. The article was so popular that he reissued it in 1907 in a separate twenty-two-page booklet and again in 1911 as part of *The Cruise of the Snark*. His following comments about the Hawaiian surf inspired many—many who brought these thoughts and surfing back to California: "Strip off your clothes that are a nuisance in this mellow clime. Get in and wrestle with the sea; wing your heels with the skill and power that reside in you; bite the sea's breakers, master them, and ride upon their backs as a king should."

Who was the first person to actually ride the Newport surf? Elliott Almond, writing for the *Los Angeles Times* in July 1989, says it was Hawaiian surfer George Freeth who tackled the waves off the Newport coast shortly after Freeth arrived on the mainland in 1907. Surfer Art Vultee compiled a handwritten list (housed in the Vultee Collection of the Surfing Heritage & Culture Center) from memory of names and dates of those who surfed Newport, Balboa and Corona del Mar. Art, a competitive swimmer who was good friends with both the Duke and George Freeth, lists Duke Kahanamoku as the first surfer to ride the breakers off Newport Beach. According to Vultee, it was in 1912, while the Duke was on his way to the Olympic Games. Freeth, Vultee recounts, was the second to enjoy the waves off Newport, in 1915. Who to believe? Sadly, we could find no primary sources to verify the dates. Local newspapers for those years either no longer exist or failed to mention the occasion.

This is a list of surfers who Art Vultee remembered surfing Newport/Balboa/Corona del Mar up to 1929.

We do know for certain that George Freeth was in the Southland before Duke Kahanamoku. Freeth had already had time to investigate the surfing conditions in the area and most likely told Kahanamoku about the surf off Newport's Corona del Mar. Though the two both claimed to be Hawaiian, they couldn't have been more different in appearance. The handsome five-foot-ten George Freeth, with doe-like brown eyes, was only a quarter Hawaiian. His father was an English sea captain (not Irish as some sources report), while his mother was half English, half Hawaiian. Kahanamoku was a full-blooded Polynesian, with dark skin and black hair. The "Duke,"

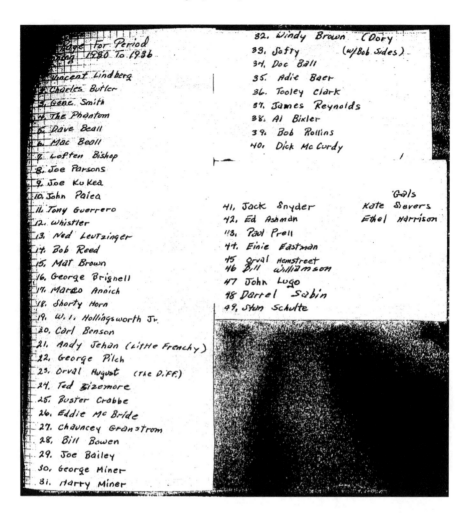

List For Period 1930 To 1936

1. Vincent Lindberg
2. Charles Butler
3. Gene Smith
4. The Phantom
5. Dave Beall
6. Mac Beall
7. Loften Bishop
8. Joe Parsons
9. Joe Kukea
10. John Paica
11. Tony Guerrero
12. Whistler
13. Ned Leutzinger
14. Bob Reed
15. Mat Brown
16. George Brignell
17. Marco Annich
18. Shorty Horn
19. W. I. Hollingsworth Jr.
20. Carl Benson
21. Andy Jehan (Little Frenchy)
22. George Pilch
23. Orval August (The D.FF.)
24. Ted Sizemore
25. Buster Crabbe
26. Eddie Mc Bride
27. Chauncey Granstrom
28. Bill Bowen
29. Joe Bailey
30. George Miner
31. Harry Miner

32. Windy Brown (Dory
33. Softy (w/Bob Sides)
34. Doc Ball
35. Adie Baer
36. Tooley Clark
37. James Reynolds
38. Al Bixler
39. Bob Rollins
40. Dick Mc Curdy

41. Jack Snyder
42. Ed Ashman
43. Paul Prell
44. Einie Eastman
45. Orval Hemstreet
46. Bill Williamson
47. John Lugo
48. Darrel Sabin
49. Stan Schulte

Gals
Kate Sievers
Ethel Harrison

This is the Vultee list from 1930 to 1936.

as Kahanamoku would be called, had been named not for Hawaiian royalty but after his father, who had been christened "Duke" following the visit of the Duke of Edinburgh to Hawaii in 1869. The younger Duke was born on August 24, 1890, in Honolulu in the same home (at King and Bishop Streets) in which Duke Sr. had first made his appearance in 1869. Like George Freeth, who was born on November 8, 1883, Duke was modest, soft-spoken, self-assured and graceful.

Both had chosen an interesting time to enter the world. King David Kalakaua was not viewed favorably by many of his people, and certain segments, such as the Hawaiian sugar interests, sought drastic changes. The

Hawaiian king's sudden death in January 1891 proved to be the catalyst for change. The king's sister, Lili'uokalani, inherited the throne, but her reign was brief. By 1893, she had been forced to abdicate because of powerful commercial factions supported by the U.S. Navy. Sanford Dole, the pineapple king, became president of the islands' provisional government. On July 4, 1894, Hawaii became a republic, presided over by President Dole. By July 7, 1898, when Duke was eight years old and George fourteen, the American flag flew over the Hawaiian Islands. Two years later, on April 30, 1900, the Organic Act made both men American citizens.

Cashing in on the success of Jack London's article on George Freeth and the new sport of surfing, Henry Huntington decided to bring Freeth to the mainland. Freeth arrived in 1907, just in time to demonstrate his skills at the opening of a consolidation of the Redondo–Los Angeles electric railroad line in Huntington's resort of Redondo Beach. Ah, if London had only traveled to Hawaii a few years earlier, perhaps George, and the sport of mainland surfing, would have been launched at Newport Beach—but that was not to be.

Freeth was an immediate success. Throngs arrived daily on Huntington's red cars to watch Freeth perform the seemingly magical feat of surfing. He also entertained visitors with an exhibition of fancy diving in the Redondo pool. He was full of new ideas. He started swimming classes, developed a variation of the trudgen stroke (a swimming stroke in which a double over-arm movement is combined with a scissors kick), and organized water polo and water basketball teams. He also helped form a surfboard-riding club in Redondo Beach in 1912, the "first organization of the kind in this country," according to the *Los Angeles Times*. The fourteen members of the club called it the Hui Nalu Club, which means "surfing club." It was named after the Hui Nalu Club of Honolulu, of which Freeth was a member.

Freeth stayed on in California to become one of the state's first lifeguards. As the area's first official lifeguard, he assembled the first volunteer lifesavings corps in Southern California and developed a cigar-shaped metal rescue kit, which he mounted on a motorcycle sidecar. After leaving Redondo, Freeth taught at Venice, giving instructions on spear fishing and surfboard riding. He became a national hero when he rescued seven Japanese fishermen during a storm in December 1908. The fishermen vowed they would never forget the heroic actions of Freeth and the lifeguards that Wednesday, December 16, 1908. Henry Huntington and his newspaper connections also ensured that the incident would not be forgotten. Having George Freeth and this new sport of surfing at his beach resort was a tourism magnet. Women

George Freeth pictured with his medal awarded for saving the lives of seven Japanese fishermen in December 1908.

loved Freeth, and men wanting female adulation and the thrill of learning a new pastime began to take up the sport of surf riding.

In 1912, Duke Kahanamoku came into the California limelight. Throughout his youth, Duke strove to refine his water skills. Swimming, surfing and canoeing were his passions. When top Australian swimmers visited the islands in 1910, Duke inspected their every move. He would use what he had learned from them to perfect his swimming skills.

It was George Freeth, the *San Diego Union-Tribune* reported in April 1919, who was instrumental in bringing Hawaiian swimmer/surfer Duke Kahanamoku to the mainland. Freeth, the article continued, was credited with teaching Kahanamoku the art of swimming in a short tank, as well as coaching him in the short dash. Sadly, thirty-five-year-old Freeth was unable to participate in the 1912 Olympics, as his amateur status was taken away because of his lifeguard salary. He had to live vicariously through his fellow Hawaiian, teaching him much of what he knew.

With Freeth's coaching, Duke's aquatic skills improved to such an extent that those who saw him were amazed. Duke's astonishing swim times were sent to the mainland, but they were so startling that officials refused to believe them. His supporters decided that the only thing they could do was raise money for Duke and another Hawaiian swimmer, Vincent Genoves, to travel to the mainland to compete for spots on the American Olympic team. The Hawaiian lads had to do much traveling, as the Olympic swim trials were held at various athletic clubs throughout the United States. On March 13, 1912, Duke won the 100-yard race in Chicago. In Pittsburgh, a short time later, Kahanamoku competed in the 220-yard indoor race and Genoves in the 500-yard indoor swimming event. Unfortunately, Duke's leg

The authors spent a number of years trying to separate the myth from the facts concerning George Freeth. Their search took them to the Huntington Library, the Los Angeles Athletic Club and archives of various newspapers, trying to find "first hand" information about Freeth. Upon visiting Greenwood Cemetery in San Diego, listed on Freeth's death certificate, the authors learned that he had been cremated and his ashes shipped to his mother, Elizabeth, in Honolulu. They had assumed that his mother had scattered his ashes in the sea he loved. In 2007, they visited Oahu Cemetery to look for other members of the Freeth family. To their amazement, they found a small cement slab next to the mother's grave with the initials G.D. (George Douglas) and his birth and death dates (1883-1919). It looks like George's mother kept his ashes (and those of a younger brother) and interred them with her (Lot #100, Section 10) when she died in 1941. Surprisingly, the cemetery had no record of George's interment.

cramped when he hit the water, and he lost the race. Neither Hawaiian would win in Pittsburgh, and only Kahanamoku would make the Olympic team and travel to Stockholm.

Duke, who almost slept through the 100-meter dash, and who had to convince officials to delay the race long enough for him to put on a swimsuit, broke the Olympic record in July 1912. He had been clocked at sixty-three and two-fifths seconds. Pandemonium ensued as the Hawaiian swimmer became a hero. He was now the most famous Hawaiian alive, and he had done much to publicize the islands.

Freeth, who hoped to show his swimming prowess in the 1916 Olympics, was disappointed once more when the 1916 games were cancelled because of World War I. He would not be around for the 1920 games. On April 7, 1919, George Freeth would die at St. Andrews's Hospital in San Diego of pneumonia brought on by influenza, his surfing legacy overshadowed by his fellow Hawaiian. Duke later called Freeth "the greatest all-round swimmer" of his day and acknowledged his own debt to Freeth's coaching skill.

Up until the completion of the jetties, the ocean and entrance to Newport Harbor were treacherous, and many lives were lost by those who tried to navigate them. But danger was nothing to Hawaiian surfer Duke Kahanamoku, who wowed spectators on Sunday, September 14, 1914, by riding the breakers at Corona del Mar, both on a surfboard and in a canoe.

Some of the onlookers had taken the Pacific Electric rail line to Balboa and crossed the bay to Corona del Mar by boat. Others had traveled the long way, by the road that had been built from Santa Ana in 1907 to accommodate the rising popularity of automobiles. The road ran from Santa Ana toward the sea, following the upper bay to the harbor and the village of Corona del Mar. (Today, the road is Back Bay Drive up to Jamboree, and then after crossing Pacific Coast Highway, it becomes Bayside Drive.) Upon reaching Corona del Mar by this circuitous route, the road ended. Only a private dirt road owned by the Irvine Company linked Newport Bay to Laguna Beach. This would change in October 1926, when the eight-mile paved Pacific Coast Highway opened a public

The South Coast Yacht Club in Newport Beach, which invited Duke Kahanamoku to visit in 1914.

gateway between the two beach communities.

On that September day, Duke was a guest of the South Coast Yacht Club (SCYC), founded in 1901, whose members proudly wore double-breasted blue coats or maroon sweaters (with SCYC on the breast) and yachting caps. The San Pedro–based club had strong connections with Hawaii, having staged the first mainland to Diamond Head race in June 1906. In April 1911, the club established Station "A" at Balboa by leasing the Pavilion. (In 1916, Dr. Albert Soilander, a member of the SCYC, would found Newport's own yacht club, the Newport Harbor Yacht Club.) It was easier to get to Newport by land rather than by sea because the breaking bar across the harbor entrance and the welter of mud flats moved about from year to year, which is how the Duke had arrived the previous afternoon. The club was honored to have the Olympic star as its guest and staged an elaborate dinner and ball in his honor.

Bay Island was home to Newport surfer Felix Modjeski. Surfing legend Duke Kahanamoku visited here in 1914. Felix Modjeski, grandson of famed Polish actress Madame Helena Modjeska, liked the beach life so much that he opened his own electrical business, drifted into real estate, became a Newport Beach electrical inspector and served as a Newport Beach city councilman from 1926 to 1928. He died in Corona del Mar on March 29, 1940, at the age of fifty-three.

At the ball, Kahanamoku spent much time talking to twenty-seven-year-old Felix Modjeski. Felix (he used the masculine form of his surname—Modjeski) was the grandson of famed Polish actress Madame Helena Modjeska, who had moved to a cottage in East Newport in 1908 from her Santiago canyon home. Felix's grandmother had died in 1909, leaving him the cottage (#3 Bay Island) and a large inheritance sufficient enough to purchase luxury items such as a surfboard.

To show his appreciation for such hospitality, the twenty-four-year-old Duke took to the water the following afternoon with fellow Hawaiian Columbus Simms and thirty-two-year-old Florence Schoneman of San Pedro. Columbus, just a year younger than Kahanamoku, was employed as a freight clerk for the Pacific Mail Service and frequently traveled with the mail between the mainland and Hawaii. Florence, a descendant of the Sepulveda family who once owned much of Southern California, was the adventurous sort who loved the water and California history. (In later years, she would do much to preserve the history of the region.)

Three launches—the *Balboa*, *Paloma* and *Apolena*—carried passengers across the bay to the beach at Corona del Mar to watch the intrepid three perform in the water. Others gathered on the cliffs and beach to view the performance. Duke, Columbus and Florence paddled out to the sandbars near the entrance to the bay, the Duke in the stern to keep the canoe straight with the breakers, which, according to the press, he did with "dexterous twists of his paddle." The three enjoyed several rides through the waves, the canoe shooting just ahead of the breakers, carrying them on a swift ride nearly a quarter of a mile.

The three eventually beached the canoe, and Kahanamoku decided to borrow a surfboard from Felix and ride the surf on Modjeski's big "log." When he got the board running right ahead of the breakers, the Duke stood up and rode inside the channel. He did this several times until he decided to thrill the crowd by sticking his feet straight up in the air and riding clear inside the channel on his head.

THE 1920s

Following his 1912 Olympic victories, Kahanamoku continued to shine. During the 1920 Olympics in Antwerp, he won gold medals in both the 100-meter and in the relay. In the 1924 Paris Olympics, he finished the 100-meter with a silver medal, the gold going to Johnny Weissmuller of Tarzan fame, and the bronze to Duke's brother, Samuel Kahanamoku.

While at the 1920 Olympics, Kahanamoku became good friends with diver and bronze-medal winner Haig Prieste, who had grown up in Long Beach, California. The two loved to joke around. On a dare, Kahanamoku persuaded Prieste to scale a flagpole at the Antwerp Games and grab the Olympic flag. Prieste, not one to back out of anything, complied, and the stolen piece of history was lost until the 103-year-old Prieste returned it to the Olympic Committee at the Sydney Games in 2000.

The two Olympic champions remained friends, and in 1921, Prieste travelled to Hawaii to learn to surf from his friend Duke Kahanamoku. The August 15, 1921 *Daily Telegram* reported:

HAIG PRIESTE HOME FROM THREE MONTHS OF HAWAIIAN TOUR: HAS MAMMOTH SURFBOARD GIVEN HIM

Haig Prieste, Olympic diving champion, returned to Long Beach with a ukulele, an oversized surfboard and an interesting story of three months in the Hawaiian Islands. He intended to remain three weeks when he left as the only American entrant in the Hawaiian carnival staged in the latter part of May. The charm of the islands, the determination to master Hawaiian surfboard riding—and the ukulele—and an opportunity to gather a couple of spare diving championships kept him several weeks overtime.

He won the junior national high-diving title and the springboard diving championship of a half dozen islands. He brought with him the Castle and Cook trophy and several others of lesser significance. He was the guest of honor and an honorary member of the Hui Nalu swimming club, the leading aquatic organization of the islands.

Prieste and Duke Kahanamoku palled around together at Hilo for a time. Prieste astonished the natives when he learned to ride the gigantic surfboards standing on his hands. "It's the greatest sport in the world," he said today.

Prieste says that the expert Hawaiian surfriders are able to ride for three-quarters of a mile on their boards. They have grown up with a surfboard in one hand, and by learning the formation of the coral reefs and the various currents, they are able to pilot their boards for great distances in a zigzag course. The waves bowl them along at a speed of 35 miles per hour. There is a great knack in catching the wave at the proper angle, Prieste says. Unless the board is pointed diagonally at the correct angle at the correct moment, both board and rider will be dumped on the coral floor of the ocean. Prieste spent from 8 to 10 hours in the water each day.

It wouldn't be long before Prieste would be testing his new wave-riding skills at Corona del Mar, according to the surfing Vultee brothers, who surfed with him there in the early 1920s.

Duke Kahanamoku, sponsored by the Outrigger Club of Honolulu, arrived on the mainland in 1922 to give public surfing demonstrations. Surfing was already so widespread that several beach communities were considering putting up signs that read "Stop, look and listen for the surfboard" and enforcing rules making all riders carry horns! With so popular a sport and so admired a star, the press followed Kahanamoku's every move. In August 1922, he was back surfing and canoeing in Newport Beach when the press caught up with him.

What was the city like back then? Balboa, at the end of the peninsula from Main to Ninth Streets, had a pavilion, a dance hall, a junky Main Street and a bunch of single-family homes and summer beach cottages. East of Main for a couple of blocks were a few houses on the bay front and a big sand beach that stretched all the way to the jetty. Farther down the peninsula at Newport was a fishing village inhabited by a couple of hundred commercial fishermen who risked their lives daily going out through the channel mouth. Balboa Island had only a dozen houses or so, hordes of mosquitoes and got pretty wet at high tide. The feeling of the rest of the town toward Balboa Island in the early days was reflected in the language of the mayor when, in 1916, the island asked to be annexed to Newport Beach. The mayor,

The community of Corona del Mar was slow to develop. This picture shows what it looked like in 1922 when surfer Duke Kahanamoku visited.

according to author Robert Gardner, responding by saying, "The island is a dump. It was sold by a lot of damn crooks to a lot of damn fools." Across the bay, at Corona del Mar, only a few homes stood on the bluff. But in 1923, further development and a need for water would add Corona del Mar territory to the city of Newport Beach. That was it. The rest of today's Newport Beach didn't exist. It was just marshland and mud flats, out of which protruded an occasional sand island, nesting places for thousands of shorebirds.

But Newport Beach had surf, which was what drew the Duke and the heavy ten-foot-long board he was riding to the area. When asked by the press about the surf, he told them that the best surf on this part of the coast was just off the Newport Harbor entrance in Corona del Mar. Here the breakers rolled in for a long distance and were strong enough to carry a surfboard satisfactorily. Kahanamoku also mentioned that he didn't like to ride the breakers at Balboa or Newport, saying they were too short and too easy. He also revealed that he was moving to Southern California and that he was going to spend a lot of time in the Newport Beach area. Among the items he was bringing from Hawaii was an outrigger canoe, which he planned on paddling from San Pedro to Balboa when it arrived. Why did he want to spend so much time here? He liked the surf at Corona del Mar and the nightlife at Balboa!

One cannot fully appreciate the flavor of the city back in the '20s and '30s without describing a typical Saturday night. Newport Beach's Balboa resembled New Orleans' Bourbon Street during Mardi Gras, and it looked like every other business establishment was involved in gambling. On March 21, 1925, a new concrete highway opened between Long Beach and Newport Beach. Before then, each of the beach towns had a paved road reaching from the town inland, but the only link between the coastal cities had been the Pacific Electric rail line. The following year, on October 9, the road opened from Newport all the way to Laguna Beach. The rush of tourists in their automobiles began!

Even after the road was completed between Corona del Mar and Laguna, surfers

> The forty-foot-wide Coast Highway, with concrete six to seven inches thick, was poured in segments that took twenty-eight days to cure. The cost of the highway was $9,500 per mile. The link connecting Newport with Laguna Beach in October 1926 made Corona del Mar easily accessible. Land sales skyrocketed.

Surfers at Corona del Mar, circa 1925. *From left to right*: Gerard Vultee, Owen Hale, Bill Herwig and Duke Kahanamoku.

who didn't have ready access to automobiles often walked between surf spots. Lorrin "Whitey" Harrison recalled those long walks and the days of surfing Corona del Mar from 1925 until 1935:

> *When I was twelve [in 1925], I started walking to Corona del Mar from Laguna Beach to go surfing. There was a crew of stand-up surfers who would ride Corona back then—Carroll Bertolet, Jack Pyle, Wally Burton, Keller Watson, Bud Higgins. Guys from Huntington Beach and all over would come to Corona del Mar because it could be just a three-foot surf, but it would pile up real high next to that jetty. We used to walk there from Laguna because there was no way to drive at the time. I didn't have a board then, but there was a bathhouse at Corona del Mar, and Duke had made a board out of white pine and left it there. There were a lot of redwoods there, too. Later on, I'd leave boards at one of the Thomas brothers' houses up on the bluff. And there was the Chinese house at China Cove. I sometimes kept my board there, too. It took us a couple hours to walk the twelve miles from Laguna Beach to Corona del Mar, but all the way was pretty nice.*

The Sparr Bathhouse in Corona del Mar was built in 1924 and used by surfers to store their boards. It became the unofficial home of the Corona del Mar Surf Club, one of the first surf clubs on the Pacific Coast.

During the Prohibition era, Harrison noted that there was nothing from Abalone Hill (near the present-day Pelican Hill golf club) except rum runners' leftover crates, boxes and bottles strewn around the beach.

Steve Farwell, a well-known local surfer in Newport Beach, fondly remembers Vincent Lindberg (also known as "Lindy" or "Klotz"), a longtime surfer who used to sit on the seawall at Blackie's surf spot and talk to Steve of bygone days. Lindy grew up in Dana Point, and each summer, a group of friends would travel up the coast to Corona del Mar by horse and wagon. They would camp on the beach and surf until their supplies ran out. They would then hide their boards by burying them in the sand and return on foot to Dana Point to get more food and whatever else they needed. This must have been in the days before the Sparr Bathhouse was built in 1924, because Captain Sheffield, who was in charge of the bathhouse, was happy to let surfers store their surfboards there free of charge.

Once Pacific Coast Highway was completed, it became easier for surfers and others to get to Corona del Mar. The author's father remembers going down there before 1936 with a paddleboard tied to the roof of the car. He had bought the board from someone who had actually rigged a small sail to it. Though he had removed the sail and the keel from the bottom, it did not work very well.

Of the 1920s, surfing icon Tom Blake wrote:

> *Often we traveled together (Duke Kahanamoku and me) to Corona del Mar, some distance south of Los Angeles, where the surf at that time was especially good. In those days of the 1920s, a long sandbar acted as a reef off the Corona del Mar beach. Over this sandbar the great storm swells would peak and break in waves up to fifteen feet high and fully a quarter of a mile offshore.*
>
> *There were never more than half a dozen surfers at a time on these expeditions to Corona del Mar. Duke was the master surf-rider; the rest of us, in comparison, were mere novices and took some terrific beatings from the breakers. We regarded Duke as our unofficial mentor.*
>
> *Among us surfing disciples of the Duke were Gerard Vultee, whose name became famous later in the field of airplane design and construction. Then there was Rusty Williams, later captain of the Los Angeles County Lifeguard Service. Still another in the group later became known as a motion-picture producer, and so on.…*

It wasn't only the surf that drew surfers to the Newport Beach area. In 1928, a newly revamped Rendezvous Ballroom, named the "Queen of Swing" in 1938 by *Look* magazine, would open its 12,000-square-foot dance floor to the public. Hordes of people flocked to Balboa, at the end of the peninsula, where liquor flowed freely despite Prohibition. Crowds surged between the Pavilion and the Rendezvous, partaking in illegal delights. With so much drinking, lots of folks went to jail. As a result, the jail built to accommodate at the most six prisoners held up to seventy-five on a busy Saturday night.

Though it was illegal statewide, gambling helped keep the City of Newport Beach afloat financially. There was a slight "technicality" in that state law allowed only for "games of skill" rather than "games of chance." As a result, a fight to prove certain games were games of skill rather than chance clogged the judicial system for years. Despite the various interpretations of what was and was not gambling, all gambling joints in Newport Beach paid a license fee to the city, and in return, city officials would alert their licensees whenever an outside police agent was in town. Once the outsider was gone, out would come the gambling tables, and Newport would go back to its sinful ways.

The Rendezvous was the place to hear the big-band sounds of the time. "Let jazz be unconfined on the beach," was the unanimous refrain of a jury

RENDEZVOUS BALLROOM

Built near this site in 1928, the Rendezvous became a showcase for Big Bands, especially during "Bal Week." For 38 years, the sounds of dance music echoed from this block-long ballroom, which was destroyed by fire in 1966. The music and dancing have ended, but the memories linger on.

Historical Site No. 36
Orange County Board of Supervisors
Orange County Historical Commission
City of Newport Beach
Placed 1986

This plaque is all that remains of the Rendezvous Ballroom.

when it brought in a verdict of "not guilty" in the case of Harry H. Tudor, manager of the original Rendezvous Ballroom, who was arrested in August 1927 on the complaint of two men who didn't like the noise. Numerous people testified that they liked the free music that drifted out of the club. The jury agreed. Music in Balboa was no crime.

The Rendezvous was originally a small dance hall located at the site of the present Balboa Theater (707 East Balboa Boulevard), competing with the Balboa Pavilion for customers. The new block-long Rendezvous made its debut on March 24, 1928, between Palm and Washington (along what is now Ocean Front Boulevard). It soon became a major West Coast venue for the touring big-band groups of the day. Before long, thousands of teenagers would come to Balboa from all over the Southland during Easter break for "Bal Week," spending days on the beach surfing and nights at the Rendezvous Ballroom partying until dawn. By the 1960s, Balboa had become the home of surf-music legend Dick Dale. In 1966, the Rendezvous would burn to the ground, ending a memorable era.

The big issue of the day for Newport Beach was how to establish a year-round economy, as the city didn't have an industry outside of fishing and illegal gambling and booze. It was hard to compete with other seaside resorts like Long Beach, which had big-pocket investors. There was another problem: the often-treacherous ocean and entrance to the harbor. In order to lure in more tourists and permanent residents, the city needed lifeguards to ensure visitor safety. Finally, after more drownings during the summer of 1923, the city hired part-time lifeguards and decided to do something about the harbor entrance. The December 26, 1923 issue of the *Long Beach Press* reported:

BEACON LIGHTS AT BALBOA ARE SET

The two beacon lights at the end of the jetty protecting the entrance of Newport Harbor are complete and have been turned over to the care of Antar Deraga, head of the Balboa lifesaving guard. The lights are about thirty feet above the ocean level and can be seen by all ships passing on the east side of Catalina.

The outer beacon light is equipped with a three-fourths-foot burner and will burn about 160 days. It flashes one second and five seconds dark. It is equipped with a sun valve for economy of operation.

The inner beacon light is equipped with a five-sixteenths-foot burner without sun valve. It should burn 200 days. This beacon flashes every two and a half seconds.

The government lighthouse service will also supply the keeper here with a lifeboat for use in rescue work. It will be in charge of Mr. Deraga, who is known as one of the most efficient lifeguards on the coast. Before coming here, he made an enviable record in Europe and has recently been made a member of the Royal lifesaving guards of England and given a service medal in recognition of heroic service in the English Channel and also for saving the life of an English lady in this harbor last summer.

Despite the signal beacons and lifeguards, Newport was fortunate to have the Duke, who had camped out on the Corona del Mar beach with some of his buddies (the Henry brothers, Bill and Tom; the Vultee brothers, Gerard and Art; Owen Hale; and Henry Chapplett), on the scene the morning of June 14, 1925. Kahanamoku proved his hero status once more. The Hawaiian swimmer was going out for his morning swim when he noticed heavy groundswells turning into tall-crested waves as they rounded the breakwater. Out in the breakwater, the forty-foot fishing yacht *Thelma* was in trouble. The boat had been chartered by a party from Riverside that had left Newport the previous morning bound for a day's fishing out at sea.

The *Thelma*, a five-ton craft partly owned by Philadelphia baseball star Gavvy Cravath, was nearing the end of the breakwater into open sea when the first groundswell loomed dead ahead. The swell, as it gained momentum, merged into a mountainous wave and crashed over the bow, smashing through the heavy plate glass of the engine room, flooding the compartment and stopping the engine. Practically all the Riverside fishermen were swept overboard with the first wave and were struggling in the midst of the torn wreckage and pounding waves. Another wave quickly followed in the wake of the first, sweeping the boat its entire length and sending rigging overboard into a maelstrom of confusion. It then pitched the boat on its side.

Encumbered by heavy clothing, the Riverside men were thrown from the boat, which started to sink almost immediately. They hadn't had time to put on life preservers before the small boat was caught broadside in the teeth of three tremendous breakers and rolled completely over three times from starboard to port on the sands of the shallow Newport sandbar. Only a few were able to reach the upturned craft and cling safely to the keel.

On the nearby beach were Duke Kahanamoku; Antar Deraga, captain of the Newport lifeguards; Charles Plummer, lifeguard; Thomas Sheffield, captain of the Corona del Mar Swimming Club; Gerard Vultee; William Herwig; and Owen Hale, who immediately went to the rescue.

Battling with his surfboard through the heavy seas, Kahanamoku was the first to reach the drowning men. He made three successive trips to the beach and carried four victims the first trip, three the second and one the third. Sheffield, Plummer and Deraga were credited with saving four men, while other members of the rescue party waded into the surf and carried the drowning men to safety as Kahanamoku brought them shoreward. Fred Hock, A. Huber, Frank Morris, Myron Bland, Fern Hock, Ellsworth Mott, William McDermott, Earl Griggs, Jack Berry, Philip Larsen, Albert Johnson and Edward Sneed were rescued, several of them near death when they were brought to shore. The drowned were William W. Squires, Riverside; Ralph Farnsworth, Riverside; John and Edgar Morris, Arlington; and E.E. McClain, father-in-law of John Morris.

Captain Porter of Newport Beach expressed the belief that at least eight or ten more would have drowned had Kahanamoku and Deraga not been ready with immediate assistance. "The Duke's performance was the most superhuman rescue act and the finest display of surfboard riding that has ever been seen in the world, I believe," he said.

When asked how he managed to rescue so many, Kahanamoku replied, "I do not know. It was done—that is the main thing. By a few tricks, perhaps."

Duke Kahanamoku, Gerard Vultee and Owen Hale (left to right) all earned awards for valor from the Los Angeles Athletic Club when they saved passengers from a capsized boat at Newport Beach.

A few days later (June 18, 1925), the Edgewater Club of Southern California announced how it was inspired by Kahanamoku's performance and "surfboard riding," which made possible the sensational rescue. Henceforth, surfboard riding would be taught on an extensive scale to members of the club. Surf riding had gained honor and respectability.

Years later, Duke Kahanamoku recalled the experience:

Big green walls of water were sliding in from the horizon, building up to bar-like heights, then curling and crashing on the shore. Only a porpoise, a shark or a sea lion had any right to be out there. From shore, we suddenly saw the charter fishing boat, the Thelma, wallowing in the water just seaward of where the breakers were falling. The craft appeared to be trying to fight her way toward safe water, but it was obviously a losing battle. You could see her rails crowded with fishermen who, at the moment, certainly had other things in mind than fishing. Mine was the only board handy right then—and I was hoping I wouldn't have to use it. It was obvious that the Thelma had capsized and thrown her passengers into the boiling sea. Neither my pals nor I were thinking heroics; we were simply running—me with a board, and the others to get their boards—and hoping we could save lives.

The Hawaiian Society of Los Angeles would present the Duke with a medal for heroism on September 4, 1925, before a large and enthusiastic assembly at the Alexander Hotel. On Christmas Day 1925, the Los Angeles Athletic Club would honor its hero with a gold watch. Thirty-two years later, three of the grateful men whose lives had been saved thanked the Duke in person before a national television audience on NBC's *This Is Your Life*. The embarrassed Duke simply replied, "That's okay."

With the newly opened portion of Coast Highway bringing more tourists, Newport Beach renewed efforts to improve its resort status and give beach visitors something else to do besides surf:

NEW "PIKE" IS PROPOSED FOR NEWPORT AREA

Announcement made today that this beach's first amusement zone will be located at Fifteenth Street, halfway between Newport and Balboa, indicates that a heretofore undeveloped area will be rapidly built up following the investment of nearly $100,000 in the project.

Prior & Church, said to be the large manufacturers of roller coasters and other thrilling play devices, have taken a ten-year lease on a plot of land 500 by 800 feet, fronting the ocean and Fifteenth Street. Prior & Church announced they will spend $65,000 at once to erect a roller coaster, which will be called the Balboa Giant Dipper. They report they already have started making cars at their shops in Venice and that work on construction will start in two weeks. The plan is to be ready for the opening May 1. — March 7, 1926 Press-Telegram

The Balboa "Fun" Zone opened in 1926 and continues to this day.

Newport Harbor entrance, late 1930s. Note that the rail tracks used to build the 1927 Peninsula jetty are still visible.

For some time, the movers and shakers in the city of Newport Beach had planned on the summer of 1928 being the greatest in its history. As mentioned earlier, the Transpacific Yacht Race to Honolulu was scheduled to leave from the harbor entrance at the end of May. The International Star races were scheduled for August, the first time they had ever been held on the West Coast. Yet there was the fiasco of the just-completed harbor "improvement." How could these races be held when the depth of the water over the sandbar in the entrance was only four feet at low tide? The time was right for a political coup. Prior to this, the political power of the City of Newport Beach lay in old Newport. After all, there were several hundred commercial fishermen permanently living there, and those votes were enough to carry any election. Balboa was merely a noisy summer resort farther down the peninsula with few full-time residents. But following the debacle of the latest jetty construction, a group of young Balboans began to plot the eventual takeover of the city, winning the city council election of 1928.

To meet this sandbar emergency, the new council formed a committee, which promptly raised $10,000 from private donations, including pennies from school children, to hire a small dredger to perform $10,000 worth of dredging. Fortunately, work was completed in time for the Memorial Day beginning of the Transpacific Race. The new city fathers thought big. Why stop with yacht racing? Since 1928 was supposed to be the most memorable year in the city's history, why not promote the first Pacific championship surf contest?

Chapter 4

Corona del Mar Surf Contests

FIRST PACIFIC COAST SURFBOARD CHAMPIONSHIPS—1928

It was Corona del Mar's Thomas Sheffield, who had allowed early surfers access to the Sparr Bathhouse to store their boards, who did all the planning and promotion for the 1928 event. The English-born journalist, swimmer and Renaissance man arrived in California in March 1915 to write a series of articles about California and Californians for the *London Daily Telegraph*. The fifty-year-old decided to stay. Age never slowed him down, and he became a swimming instructor at the Los Angeles Athletic Club, competed in numerous swimming competitions and in his spare time worked with the Red Cross. In 1924, he was hired by William Sparr to design and manage Sparr's $50,000 bathhouse in Corona del Mar.

Along with architect Holmes Paul, Sheffield, an eminent authority on bathhouses, envisioned

The first Southern California surfboard contest was held on July 25, 1914, in Seal Beach during the Minnesota State Society annual picnic. The *Los Angeles Times* described it as "the first of its kind on the coast." Contestants started twenty-five yards from shore, where the waves were breaking best, and made a dash to shore, the winner being the "surfer" who first reached the beach on the crest of a large wave. Unfortunately, no mention was made of the winner of that historic contest.

The Sparr Bathhouse was built to promote sales for William Sparr's real estate ventures in Corona del Mar, including Balboa Bay Palisades, as this July 15 1923 *Press Telegram* ad shows.

an Old English–style structure. It would accommodate four hundred bathers and furnish them with every modern convenience, including showers, footbaths, hair dryers and a day nursery for babies. Surrounding the bathhouse, a resort was planned that included a café (with an adjoining ice-cream parlor) situated on a one-hundred-foot veranda, commanding a picturesque view of the ocean. On the recreational grounds on the cliffs above the bathhouse there would be tennis, volley and handball, a bowling alley, archery, a shooting gallery, deck games and other forms of amusement. The bathhouse was to be the first unit of one of the most extensive developments on the coast. According to the July 27, 1924 *Los Angeles Times*, it would also include an exclusive $500,000 Corona del Mar Club, as well as the $75,000 Sea Cove Village, which was to consist of forty-eight cottages, a reception hall, a dance pavilion and playgrounds.

Sparr, a Los Angeles fruit packer and real estate developer, had purchased Corona del Mar from the F.D. Cornell Company in 1922, according to Corona del Mar historian Douglas Westfall. Sparr had great hopes for this real estate venture, which included new developments such as Balboa Bay Palisades and the resort of Sea Cove Village. The Balboa Bay Palisades, launched in July 1923, was two hundred yards from the shoreline of the bay and four hundred yards from the beaches on the ocean side. Both the Bay Palisades and Sea Cove Village had great potential, Sparr believed, as the new Coast Highway would cut through the property, allowing easy access for tourists to his resort and an instant increase in the value of his properties.

So far, development of this area of the coast had been a dismal failure. The F.D. Cornell Company had traded land in Riverside County to Corona del Mar founder George Hart in February 1915. The property comprised practically all of the unsold land in Corona del Mar, including about four hundred acres divided into more than 2,200 building lots. The property, renamed Balboa Palisades, was part of a seven-hundred-acre tract bought by George Hart from James Irvine ten years earlier. Since its founding in 1905, Hart had managed to build only one small hotel and fifteen houses. One of the fifteen houses belonged to the Everett family, who built a summer cottage in Corona del Mar in 1910. In 1917, the Everetts traveled to Honolulu, where thirteen-year-old Boyd became so enamored with surfing that he brought a solid mahogany surfboard back to Corona del Mar with him. His sister Mary, in her memoir, said he was the first person she ever saw ride the waves off the Corona del Mar bluff.

Why so few land sales in such a beautiful location? One reason was lack of water—something William Sparr quickly remedied by having Corona del Mar annexed to Newport Beach (and Newport's water supply) in April 1923. Having the Pacific Coast Highway extended past Newport in 1926 was also anticipated to help sales. But Sparr's grandiose plans for Corona del Mar ran into a snag in September 1924. Sparr's petition to the Newport

Beach Board of Trustees to narrow the width of Ocean Drive from 110 to 50 feet and to abandon streets leading down to the beach to allow him to erect an exclusive club on the property was denied on the grounds that the abandonment of the streets would forever exclude the public from the beach. Sparr had already built a bathhouse and dance pavilion on the sands below the Corona del Mar cliffs at a cost of $50,000 and hired Thomas Sheffield to run the bathhouse, proposed club and Sea Cove Village.

Sparr bided his time. In June 1925, he announced a revised plan for his clubhouse—the $150,000 Balboa Palisades Club. The three-story structure would be of Spanish design and include several private dining rooms, a pool room, a smoking room, guest rooms (practically all with private baths) and a bowling alley in the basement. In October 1925, with a host of celebrities including Duke Kahanamoku present, the cornerstone was laid. However, in July 1926, with Corona del Mar soon to open to the outside world following the completion of the Pacific Coast Highway, Sparr put all of the water frontage, bluff lots and 350 lots on top of the Palisades up for sale. In October 1926, the Balboa Palisades Club was taken over by a group of Pasadena, Los Angeles, Riverside and Whittier businessmen, who planned to finish the

In 1938, a false second story was put on the Sparr Bathhouse for the movie *Spawn of the North*, as Corona del Mar was transformed into Ketchikan, Alaska. The cinematography and sound effects won a special Academy Award. Damaged in a fire in the early 1940s, the bathhouse was never rebuilt.

structure and begin the bungalows envisioned in Sparr's Sea Cove Village. The economic depression that struck America in 1929 resulted in another change in ownership, as the club was taken over by Caltech with funds from lumber and electricity baron William Kerckhoff to create a beachfront lab. Today, you can still visit this piece of Corona del Mar history, located at 101 Dahlia Street.

Sparr had chosen well in selecting Thomas Sheffield to run things. Besides his other talents, Sheffield was a good PR man. Knowing the popularity of Olympic medalist Duke Kahanamoku and the growing sport of surfing, he publicized the likeness of Corona del Mar's beach to that of Waikiki and offered space in Sparr's bathhouse for the Duke and his friends to store their heavy surfboards. Though there would be no exclusive $500,000 Corona del Mar Club, there would be the $150,000 Balboa Palisades Club, as well as a club of a different sort—the Corona del Mar Surf Club. Having the surfers at Corona attracted tourists and potential real estate buyers. It was a good combination, and in 1928, Sheffield saw an opportunity he could not pass up. With the International Star yacht races taking place, why not hold the first Pacific Coast Surfboard contest in Corona del Mar at the same time?

This is what the July 16, 1928 *Press-Telegram* had to say about the surfing event:

SURFBOARD CLUB WILL HOLD TITLE MEET AT HARBOR

The Corona del Mar Surfboard Club, which claims to be the largest organization of its kind in the world, will hold a championship surfboard riding tournament at the Corona del Mar beach at the entrance to Newport Harbor on Sunday, August 5.

Some of the most notable surfboard riders in the world are expected to compete, including the famous swimmer and surfboard rider Duke Kahanamoku, Hawaiian champion; Tom Blake of Redondo, who won two championships; and Harold Jarvis, long-distance swimmer of the Los Angeles Athletic Club. Some of the surfboard riders are predicting that new world records will be made here during the meet. So far, fifteen surfboard artists have signed up, including some from as far away as San Francisco. It is planned to make it an annual event.

On August 5, 1928, the Corona del Mar Surf Club, twelve wooden boards strong, and Thomas Sheffield hosted the first Pacific Coast surfboard competitions. In addition, there were contestants from Santa Monica, Redondo and Los Angeles, making a total of fifteen entries.

AN INVITATION
TO - YOU - OF
"Orange County"
SPEND THE DAY WITH US

AT THE

"Corona Del Mar Beaches"
ON EAST SIDE OF NEWPORT BAY

BRING YOUR PICNIC BASKETS—PLENTY OF CLEAN SAND BEACH

NEXT SUNDAY AUGUST 5th

Pacific Coast Surf Board Championship

The Meet Is Under the Auspices of the

Famous Corona del Mar Surf Board Club

Largest Club of this class in America. Its membership includes such world famous figures as Duke Kahanamoku, Tom Blade of Redondo, Gerrard Vultee, Art Vultee of the Los Angeles Athletic Club, Clyde Swedson, Swimming Coach to the Hollywood Athletic Club; L. Jarvis, R. Williams, H. Hutchinson and many other famous experts in Surf Board Riding.

REFEREE—Mr. L. Henry, Los Angeles Athletic Club
STARTER—Capt. T. W. Sheffield

ALL ORANGE COUNTY FOLKS WILL BE THERE SUNDAY

ALL ORANGE COUNTY FOLKS WILL HAVE A GOOD TIME

FIRST EVENT 12:00 M.

1.—PADDLING RACE ACROSS BALBOA CHANNEL FROM CORONA DEL MAR BEACH TO JETTY AND BACK.
2.—CANOE TILTING CONTEST.
3.—DEMONSTRATION OF LIFE SAVING BY SURF BOARDS. (Members of the Club rescued fifteen men off the Thelma when she capsized in a rough surf.)
4.—THRILLING ROUGH WATER SURF BOARD RACE FROM BELL BUOY TO CHANNEL NEAREST EAST JETTY.

Prizes Donated by W. S. Sparr, H. Bowman, Balboa Palisades Club, T. W. Sheffield, The Dyas Co., Los Angeles and Hollywood

THE PRIZES WILL BE PRESENTED TO THE WINNERS BY MAYOR JOHNSON OF NEWPORT BEACH

Races Commence Fifteen Minutes After the First Aerial Bomb at 12:30 P. M. on the West Beach of Rocky Point, Corona del Mar. The Rough Water Surf Board Race Commences from the East Beach following the Paddling Races.

REMEMBER—
Corona del Mar
REMEMBER—
THIS "PROGRAM" IS ABSOLUTELY FREE

THEN - TOO—
YOU WILL SEE OTHER WONDERFUL SIGHTS DURING TH DAY, SUCH AS THE SPEED BOATS "WHIZZING" BY—THE AIR SHIPS—THE SAILBOATS—THE BEAUTIFUL YACHTS GOIN IN AND OUT—THE FISHERMEN WITH THEIR CATCH — TH "BATHERS" ENJOYING THE "STILL WATER" AND "SURF", TH "GROUPS" ALONG THE BEACHES, HAVING—

A WONDERFUL TIME

DIRECTIONS
FROM THE ARCHES SOUTH. FOUR MILES TO MARGUERITE AVENUE ON STATE HIGHWAY

An invitation to the first Pacific Coast Surfboard Championship.

The competitions included a paddling race across Balboa channel from Corona del Mar beach to the Peninsula jetty and back, a canoe tilting contest, a demonstration of the use of surfboards in saving lives and a thrilling rough-water surfboard race from the bell buoy to the channel nearest the Peninsula jetty. The *Press-Telegram* reported:

PLANS COMPLETED FOR SURFBOARD RIDING TILT

Preparations have been completed for the Pacific Coast surfboard riding championship tournament, to be held at Corona del Mar, the entrance to Newport Harbor today. Part of the entrance to the harbor is said to be surpassed only by some Hawaiian beaches for surfboard riding.

Duke Kahanamoku and other well-known surfboard artists will compete. Besides surfboard riding, the program will include canoe-tilting contests, paddling races and a life-saving exhibition by surfboard riders. In addition to Kahanamoku, other well-known members of the club include Tom Blake of Redondo, Gerard Vultee and Art Vultee of the Los Angeles Athletic Club, Clyde Swedson of the Hollywood Athletic Club, and others.

Though Duke Kahanamoku was expected to attend, the filming of his latest movie, *The Rescue*, prevented him from making the event. This left the field open to a new generation of surfers. The course for the "thrilling rough-water surfboard race" was to paddle out to a buoy, five hundred yards offshore, and then ride a wave back to the beach. Whoever made it back first was the winner. Fifteen competitors vied for victory in this first competition. With the event being so new, there were few rules set in place, and Tom Blake won the contest by taking out two boards, putting one on top of another. The bottom board was really a paddleboard. It was fifteen feet long, nineteen inches wide and four inches thick. Weighing in at 110 pounds, it was his own creation, which he called the "Hawaiian Hollow Surfboard." Paddling both boards, the smaller on top of the larger, Tom was first to reach the buoy. He then switched from the longer paddleboard to the shorter surfboard, leaving the paddleboard behind and winning the race.

In 1928, a board strictly for paddling was unheard of. Everyone competed in paddling races on "regular" wave-riding surfboards. Before World War I, George Freeth had designed an eight-foot-long, twenty-four-inch-wide, two-foot-thick redwood board weighing about forty pounds to teach beginner surfers, but up until 1924, the ten-foot redwood plank that Duke Kahanamoku and early Waikiki surfers had ridden since around 1900 was most commonly used. In 1926, Hawaiian Lorrin Thurston came into the picture by crafting a twelve-foot board out of balsa wood. These ten- to twelve-foot boards were found along the coast until Tom Blake's designs arrived on the scene.

The true Messiah of surfboard manufacturing was Tom Blake, who forever changed the course of board design. During the next few years, many surfers on the coast began turning in their old spruce, pine and redwood solid boards for lighter, faster, Blake-style hollow paddleboards and surfboards. Others, however, refused to embrace the hollow board design. Even later, when hollow boards became the standard at many beaches, solid boards were still in use.

Tom used the hollow board not only for the surfing contest but also for the paddling contest held that same day. He won both. The paddleboard he used in the competition was a good four feet longer than any of the other boards. It was also narrower, making it possible to get a deeper arm stroke in the water with each paddle.

For the surfboard race, Tom knew that Gerard Vultee had the upper hand with his eleven-foot-long board. The longer board, built on the Corona del Mar beach by Duke Kahanamoku, gave Vultee a speed advantage. There

Waikiki VII

was little doubt that Gerard would be the first one out to the buoy, marking the surf break, and therefore the first to get a wave back in and win the event. Seeing this obvious advantage, Tom decided to use the longer hollow board, which he had brought for the paddling event, in the surf race. There were no rules on how many boards you could take out at one time, so he simply placed the smaller surfboard on top of the longer paddleboard. To paraphrase Blake's recollections of that day:

Blake brought both this hollowed-out paddleboard and a nine-foot-six-inch redwood board with him by ship to the mainland in 1928. They were both painted white, with the name "Waikiki III" on the paddleboard and "Waikiki VII" on the surfboard.

I had them both on the beach as the starting gun went off. Everybody got a good head start…Vultee in the lead. I slowly proceeded to put the 15-foot paddleboard in the water—then went back to get the 9 ½ job, placed it upon the paddleboard and started after the field, now 50 yards out. I slowly caught and passed them at 300 yards and arrived at the bell buoy alone with a minute to spare. I discarded the paddleboard and lined up for the first wave. The waves were 6 or 7 feet high—not large, but strong.

Gerard Vultee was the first to arrive after Tom; the rest followed. They all had to wait a few minutes for a set of waves. When the first good set appeared, Tom discarded his large hollow board, taking off on his smaller board, with Gerard in hot pursuit. Vultee claimed the wave and took off for shore. But the second wave was a bit bigger, and Tom headed in the other direction. Vultee's wave petered out in the channel while Tom's carried him all the way to shore for the win.

Gerard Vultee and the board made by Duke Kahanamoku for the 1928 Pacific Coast Surfboard Competition.

Surfers gather below the cliffs at Corona del Mar for the first Pacific Coast Surfboard Competition, 1928.

Tom Blake recalled there being a newsreel crew on shore to record this historic surfing event. They caught his ride on camera, and he later had a close-up made from the film. Unfortunately, Tom lost track of the still shot.

It's interesting to note that the advantage the hollow board gave Tom in paddling out to the break evaporated once he got there. There were no waves coming in at the time, so the other competitors were able to catch up to him. The hollow board weighed 110 pounds, and Tom's regular surfboard would have weighed at least 50 pounds. Together, he was paddling a weight of 160 pounds or more. The extra board width, combined with the additional thickness of the two boards, would have meant that he could not get his arms down into the water to paddle very well. It is an amazing testament to his ability that he beat any of the other contestants out to the buoy.

It's important to note that Tom's "edge" in all the paddling contests he participated in during his long career was not due solely to his innovative paddleboard designs—he was also a gifted paddler. This natural ability showed in the 1928 contest when he was able to catch a wave right after Gerard Vultee's, even though his board was at least one and a half feet shorter than Vultee's or any of the other competitors'.

Contestants line up at Corona del Mar for the 1928 contest.

Tom also won the paddling race across the channel and back using the hollow board. He let Vultee lead for most of the race but breezed by him on the experimental paddleboard.

For his two wins, Tom received a statue of a swimmer and a silver cup. He kept the statue but donated the cup to be used as a perpetual trophy in future Pacific Coast surf contests.

Tom was also involved with Captain Sheffield of the Sparr Bathhouse in planning the contest's events. Since this was the first surfing contest, the men were tasked with determining what exactly a surf contest was to include and how it was to be won. In his *Hawaiian Surf Riders* (1935), Tom included this quote from the *American Anthropologist* (1889): "Racing in the surf is called *hei-hei-na-lu*, from *hei-hei*, meaning 'to race,' and *nalu*, meaning 'surf.' Two champions will swim out to sea on boards, and the one first arriving on shore wins." It is probable that this historical reference gave Tom the idea for the combination paddling-and-wave-riding event.

This is one of the rare pictures of Tom Blake's 1928 trophy, taken by Doc Ball for his book *California Surfriders*, published in 1946. Winners since 1928 are inscribed on the back of the trophy: 1928—Tom Blake; 1929—Keller Watson; 1932—Preston Peterson; 1934—Gardner Lippincott; 1936—Preston Peterson; 1938—Preston Peterson; 1939—Lorrin Harrison; 1940—Cliff Tucker; 1941—Preston Peterson. Unfortunately, the current whereabouts of the trophy are unknown.

Tom also had much to say about Newport Beach surf conditions in *Hawaiian Surf Riders*. The "Balboa" Blake describes is really what we refer to in this book as Corona del Mar. Tom stated:

> *Waikiki is not the only place in the world that surf is ridden. The single other known place is Balboa, California. Good riding surf is much more*

consistent at Balboa, California, than at Waikiki. Duke first rode there 20 years ago; today, some 15 or 20 boys enjoy the sport in the summer time mostly, and even then the water is so cold a half hour surfing sends one to shore to shiver for the rest of the day. However, Balboa surf is more reliable or consistent than Waikiki surf. On a good day, I have ridden four hundred yards; that lets you right on the sand, and a longer ride is impossible.

We've heard from Tom Blake, the big winner of the day. But what did the press have to say about the day's activities? Here's an example from the August 6, 1928 *Press-Telegram*:

LOS ANGELES MAN, TOM BLAKE, WINNER OF EVENTS OF SURFBOARD CLUB

The aquatic powers of Tom Blake, bewhiskered athlete of the Los Angeles Athletic Club, enabled him to win over an assemblage of swimmers in the meet held yesterday afternoon in front of the Sparr Bathhouse on the Corona del Mar beach. Blake took two of the first places, winning easily the surfboard contest and the paddling race. He was awarded silver trophies for his championship.

Several hundred people lined the beach to witness the contest held under the auspices of the Corona del Mar Surfboard Association. The fact that Duke Kahanamoku, famous surfboard rider, could not be present did not detract from the excitement of the day.

The Corona del Mar Surfboard Club has been sponsored by Captain T.W. Sheffield, manager of the Sparr Bathhouse. It is said to be the only organization of its kind on the Pacific Coast.

The results of the contest were as follows: Quarter-mile surfboard race, won by Tom Blake, L.A.A.C.; second, Gerard Vultee, Corona del Mar; third, Dennie Williams, Corona del Mar. Paddling race was won by Tom Blake; second, Dennie Williams.

The canoe-tilting event was won by a team composed of R. Eaill and E. Fry, who beat brothers Paul and Jack Beckett.

Did you know there are six wave types along the coast of Southern California? According to a University of California study, the wave varieties are based on where they are generated and include Aleutian low, Pineapple Express, Northwest swell, Tropical storm, Southern Hemisphere swell and Local sea breezes.

SECOND PACIFIC COAST SURFBOARD CHAMPIONSHIPS—1929

Realizing the success of the 1928 contest, Sheffield cashed in on the popularity of surfing and held a second event on September 5, 1929. The September 12, 1929 *Balboa Times* reported on the competition:

CORONA DEL MAR WINS FAME IN SURFBOARD RACE

Newport Bay and Orange County will gain national and international publicity as a result of the surfboard races held at Corona del Mar beach Sunday when some of the most famous surfboard rulers of the West competed for trophies at the entrance channel of Newport Harbor.

Seldom has any event been held on any part of the Bay been attended by so many. This is because the Corona del Mar Surfboard Club, under whose auspices the races were held, is said to be the only club of its kind on the North American continent and the local harbor entrance is regarded as next to Hawaii for surfboard riding.

Grant Leenhouts of Redondo won the surfboard paddling race and Keller Watson of Orange the standing surfboard race, thereby obtaining handsome silver put up by Capt. T.W. Sheffield. Houghton Ralph of Corona del Mar was second in the surfboard paddling race and Keller Watson third. Gerard Vultee of the Los Angeles Athletic Club finished second in the standing surfboard contest, with Gordon Thomas third.

Grant Leenhouts was a Palos Verdes Swimming Club lifeguard whose daring rescue of a fisherman in August 1933 made news. Leenhouts would go on to make 3,700 war films during World War II. Houghton Ralph, a Hermosa Beach lifeguard, would also attract media attention when, in May 1934, he helped rescue six swimmers in almost the same number of minutes. Gerard Vultee, who graduated from the UCLA School of Engineering in 1920, went into aviation, starting the Airplane Development Corporation in 1932 and Vultee Aircraft. Sadly, he would die in a plane crash in 1938. His aircraft company would continue, eventually becoming part of McDonnell Douglas in 1994.

Keller Watson was a newcomer to surfing, he told *Los Angeles Times* reporter Elliott Almond in 1989. Watson's family had summered in Newport Beach in 1928, at which time twenty-one-year-old Keller was amazed to see people riding wooden planks on the long breakers at Corona del Mar. He swam across the channel and met the "in" group from the Corona del Mar Surf Club. There was Whitey Harrison and his sister Ethel, who made white canvas swim trunks ideal for bodysurfing; Matt Brown, who later owned a Santa Ana bookstore; Barney Klotz, Mac "Laho Leo" Beal; Sol "Crazy Nel" Kalami; and Gene "Tarzan" Smith. Though he had earned a degree in pharmacy from USC, Watson was so in love with beach life that he and his pals ran a hot dog stand on the beach before the Corona break went away.

Watson was hooked on surfing. His winning wave in 1929 was estimated as a ten-footer, though breakers off Corona del Mar often reached heights of twenty feet. Watson remembered that his friend Mac Beal once broke three surfboards on the jetty in three hours and that all he could do was watch as they washed in and smashed against the rocks.

Little did those who participated in the 1929 contest know that the world was soon to change. As the 1920s neared an end, many were convinced that prosperous times would go on forever. On September 3, 1929, stock prices reached their highest level yet, but a slow decline began. On October 24, an abrupt dip led bankers to attempt stemming the tide. On October 29, Black Tuesday, a record 16,410,030 shares were traded, as huge blocks of stock were dumped for whatever they would bring. By December 1, stocks on the New York Stock Exchange had dropped in value by $26 billion. The

Thomas Sheffield (in white) prepares participants for the start of the 1928 Pacific Coast Surfboard Championship. Note the onlookers sitting on the concrete Corona del Mar jetty.

day after the crash, President Herbert Hoover assured the public that the business of the country was on a sound and prosperous basis. In actuality, the Great Depression of the 1930s had begun.

In May 1930, sixty-five-year-old surfing promoter Thomas Sheffield saw the veneer begin to crumble. Churches were asked to open their doors and give homeless men a night's lodging. Fort MacArthur in San Pedro furnished one hundred cots and bedding for the itinerant men who had come to seemingly prosperous Southern California looking for work. Property sales in Corona del Mar had plummeted, and no buyers meant no money in Sheffield's pockets. The Balboa Palisades Club had been sold to Caltech and had no use for him. He decided to take a friend's offer and manage an estate in Santa Monica, subsequently resigning from his Sparr Bathhouse post in Corona del Mar. His leaving meant that there would be no Pacific Coast surfboard contest in 1930 or 1931.

Sheffield would continue to lead an active life. On January 1, 1952, the eighty-seven-year-old emerged from the fifty-six-degree water and found five lovely young ladies from Janet Dee's Surfboard Ballet bearing towels with which to dry him. This New Year's Day swim was a rite he had practiced for over thirty years but the first with pretty girls waiting to greet him. And it would be his last. Thomas Sheffield died on December 19, 1952, just a few weeks short of his anticipated 1953 New Year's Day swim.

THIRD PACIFIC COAST SURFBOARD CHAMPIONSHIPS—1932

Not all was doom and gloom during the Depression years, especially among young folk. In 1931, Bal Week began in Balboa, with students from all over Southern California taking over the peninsula during Easter break. Why choose Balboa in Newport Beach? One reason was surfing—the other? Easy access to illegal booze.

However, by the end of 1933, Prohibition would be no more, and Newport Beach would take on a more "honorable" persona. But surfing would continue. By the early 1930s, there were as many as two hundred regular surfers in Southern California, exploring every inlet, cove and beach in search of new and better waves. Newport Beach surfers were proud of having what the May 17, 1931 *Press-Telegram* called "the only real Hawaiian surfboard club on the California coast." Conditions at the harbor entrance channel were such that huge groundswells formed nearly a half mile from shore on the outside of the Corona del Mar jetty, allowing surfers to spend many hours riding the combers. Why not take advantage of such conditions and hold another surf contest? In an attempt to boost tourism, Newport Beach again hosted the Pacific Coast Surfboard Championships in September 1932. With Captain Sheffield gone, other "old time" surfers—Felix Modjeski, Antar Deraga and Art Vultee—stepped up to the plate to do the planning. They convinced the Newport Harbor Chamber of Commerce to sponsor the September 25, 1932 event at Corona del Mar.

Fourteen surfers from around Southern California gathered that day. Judges included Antar Deraga, former Newport Beach lifeguard who went on to become an airplane pilot; Art Vultee, who earned a degree in steam engineering, working in the shipyards during World War I and II and later in the automobile business; and Felix Modjeski, former city councilman. Besides surfboard riding and bodysurfing, the day's events also included exhibition kayak races and a rough-water swim for girls.

The surfboard contest started the day. The course led from the outer end of the Corona del Mar jetty in toward the bay. The first surfer to finish three complete rides the length of the Corona jetty was the winner, and it was Preston "Pete" Peterson, a Santa Monica lifeguard, who won first place in the two-hundred-yard contest. Allen Hunt of Sunset Beach came in second, while Wally Burton of Los Angeles came in third.

In the afternoon, the surfboard-paddling contest was held. All were hoping to beat the Hawaiian record of 31.25 seconds for the one-hundred-yard race and four minutes forty-nine seconds for the half-mile. Three Santa Monicans—nineteen-year-old Pete Peterson, twenty-two-year-old Chauncey Granston and twenty-one year-old Wally Burton—were first, second and third in both the one-hundred-yard and half-mile races. Peterson won the first race in 28.2 seconds and the second in 4 minutes 59.3 seconds. He had bested the Hawaiian record in the one-hundred-yard race but didn't have enough left in him to also take the half-mile record. However, Peterson would continue to dominate the Pacific Coast Surfboard Championships up until World War II, winning four out of the nine competitions (1932, 1936, 1938 and 1941).

Newport Beach teenager Helen Huffman wowed spectators by doing the "barrel roll," turning around like a barrel without using any arm strokes, and several other stunts while competing in the bodysurfing contest. Sixteen-year-old Helen was one of five women who competed. She came in first, seventeen-year-old Ethel Harrison of Anaheim came in second and Helen Harper of Orange came in third. Ted Sizemore of

Huntington Park won the men's bodysurfing event, with Don Brown of Laguna Beach and thirteen-year-old Charles Carey of Huntington Park coming in second and third, respectively.

The year 1933 was one that Newport Beach would never forget. On March 4, 1933, a huge crowd gathered around radios to listen to the inauguration of a new president, Franklin Delano Roosevelt. Roosevelt was quick to act to get the country on its feet again. On March 6, 1933, in order to keep the banking system of the country from collapsing, FDR used the powers given by the Trading With the Enemy Act of 1917 and suspended all transactions in the Federal Reserve and other banks and financial institutions. On March 9, Congress met in a special session and passed the Emergency Banking Relief Act. This gave the president the power to reorganize all insolvent banks and provided the means by which sound banks could reopen their doors without long delay. As Roosevelt was "shaking up" the financial community, Newport Beach (and all of Southern California) experienced a shaking up of its own.

At 5:54 p.m. on the evening of March 10, 1933, the ground around Newport shook for eleven seemingly never-ending seconds. The killer-force quake, measuring 6.3 on the Richter scale, killed over 140 people throughout the Southland. Fortunately, the quake, centered off Newport, did little damage due to the fact that the sand seemed to act as a buffer and left most of the buildings intact. It's somewhat ironic that the sand they were trying to get rid of in the bay actually saved lives and property!

THE MYSTERY PACIFIC COAST CHAMPIONSHIP CONTESTS 1934 AND 1936

While the young were surfing, the oldsters were at work "improving" Newport Bay. At first, the Depression made any harbor improvements seem a dead issue. But local businessman George Rogers took it upon himself to travel to Washington, D.C., and lobby for federal funds to dredge Newport Bay. He succeeded in getting all but $640,000 of a $1,835,441 harbor project. Back in Orange County, Rogers and city engineer Richard Patterson managed to convince Orange County voters to finance the balance. On Sunday, September 23, 1934, Newport Harbor construction was launched with the placing of the first barge of rock at the end of the Peninsula jetty. The day was one of celebration, including a huge aquatic event.

It's thanks to early surf photographer John Heath "Doc" Ball that we know surf contests were actually held in 1934 and 1936. In his 1946 book *California Surfriders*, Ball lists Gardner Lippincott as winning the contest in 1934 and Pete Peterson the winner in 1936. Born in Los Angeles in 1907, Doc Ball followed in his father's footsteps and became a dentist. He opened a dental office in 1934 that also became a hangout for his surf buddies from the Palos Verdes Surf Club. Doc had been drawn to photography in 1931 and took it upon himself to capture the surfing lifestyle that was growing throughout California. The surfing community of today owes much to this man, who passed away in December 2001 at the age of ninety-four.

Piecing together various sources, including Ball's reference to the event and newspaper articles of the time, we believe that the 1934 Pacific Coast Surfboard Championship could have taken place in conjunction with the September 23, 1934 launch of the jetty construction in Newport Harbor. Though we have not been able to find any direct reference to surfing in newspaper articles of the time, we do know a large aquatic celebration, sponsored by the Newport Harbor Recreational Commission, was held that day. It included a two-mile rough-water swim between Balboa Pier and Newport Pier, and an ocean kayak race. Was surfing included? We can't say for sure, but it seems that local surfers may have realized their days of surfing Corona del Mar were numbered and had participated in the aquatic celebration.

What of the 1936 Pacific Coast Surfboard competition? Could this have been the final surfing contest held at Corona Del Mar? We do know from Whitey Harrison that surfers didn't let the dredging stop them from enjoying the waves. As the dredging was going on, surfers kept surfing in the channel. Could they have had one final fling sometime in 1936? Or had they already abandoned Corona for San Onofre?

Whitey Harrison told *Los Angeles Times* reporter Elliott Almond that he remembered a day in 1935 when Corona del Mar's waves became so dismal that the surfers packed three carloads of friends and drove to San Onofre. After their discovery of good waves there, they never returned to Corona del Mar. They wanted a remote place where they wouldn't run into boats or swimmers. San Onofre met the bill. So, conceivably, the 1936 contest could have been held at San Onofre—or perhaps somewhere else. We just don't know. All we know is that the year and the winner's name was inscribed on the perpetual Pacific Coast Surfboard trophy photographed by Doc Ball and shown in his book *California Surfriders*.

It was local Newport businessman George Rogers who lobbied for federal funds to dredge Newport Bay. Known as the father of Newport Harbor, the sixty-one-year-old would die of a heart attack in July 1936 aboard his yacht *Memory* in almost the same spot where his son George Jr. had drowned a few years earlier.

Sadly, the days of having surf competitions at Corona del Mar came to an end. The harbor "improvements" of 1934–36 would create a safe harbor but end the wave action that had made Corona del Mar another Waikiki. Jetty work began in the fall of 1934, and by 1935, surfing was all but lost when the jetties were lengthened, obstructing the waves. One benefit, however, of the longer Corona jetty was that the beach at Corona del Mar was extended about two hundred feet seaward, and the city of Newport Beach obtained nearly one thousand feet of ocean and bay frontage for public use.

On May 23, 1936, the new harbor would open amid much fanfare. The May 20, 1936 edition of the *Press-Telegram* noted:

NEWPORT HARBOR TO NOTE OPENING

Headed by a picturesque Spanish adventure ship, a parade of more than 1,000 yachts and pleasure boats representing all ports of the Pacific Coast will stream into Newport Harbor Saturday. The great parade of boats will enter the harbor on a signal received from President Franklin D. Roosevelt at Washington. A Coast Guard cutter will fire the signal guns, which will start the parade at 1 p.m. Two divisions of boats, one including small craft, cruisers and sailboats and the other including big yachts, will form the water caravan which will wend its way into the harbor.

The Spanish ship San Salvador, under command of Juan Rodriguez-Cabrillo, discoverer of California, and Vasco Nunez de Balboa, discoverer of the Pacific, will anchor in the Balboa Basin. Aboard the boat will be Father Neptune and the royal court made up of the prettiest girls of twelve Southern California cities. City and County officials of Southern California communities and Governors of three States and Lower California will board the boat and welcome Father Neptune to the port.

A daylight fireworks display at 2 p.m., the firing of an official salute to Governor Frank F. Merriam at 3 p.m. and an official inspection tour of the harbor by the Governor will complete the afternoon program. Batteries of Army searchlights will illuminate the harbor district starting at 8 p.m. and at 9 p.m. a second fireworks display. The celebration will continue Sunday with another big parade of boats.

It would never become a major commercial harbor as envisioned twenty years earlier, but Newport Beach would continue with commercial fishing and boat building. It began to attract the affluent yachting set, including several film stars such as Errol Flynn, Humphrey Bogart, Dick Powell, James Cagney and Leo Carrillo, all of whom owned yachts in Newport Bay.

Chapter 5

Goodbye Corona del Mar: Other Surf Contest Locations

S urfing competitions were growing in popularity, though the rules in each contest could vary. On July 28, 1935, nearby Huntington Beach held its first Aquatic Sports Day program, which included surfboard riding, breaker riding, a kayak race, a long paddleboard race and a swim around the pier. The day's events were held back a bit when two thirteen-year-old girls fell over the pier railing just as the breaker-riding contest was set to begin!

Sixth–Ninth Pacific Coast Surfboard Championships
1938–1941

Though the Corona del Mar Surf Club was no more, it had inspired the formation of other surf clubs throughout Southern California. The Pacific Coast Surfboard contest continued under various names with Gardner Lippincott winning in 1934; Pete Peterson in 1936, 1938 and 1941; Whitey Harrison in 1939; and Cliff Tucker in 1940.

As already mentioned, we haven't been able to find anything definitive about the 1934 or 1936 contest, which may have been held in either Corona del Mar, San Onofre or somewhere else, but the exodus of surfers from Corona del Mar to San Onofre (or "Nofre," as the surfers called it) resulted in San Onofre becoming the preferred location for the 1938 Pacific Coast Surfboard contest.

1938 Pacific Coast Surfboard Champions. *From left to right*: Pete Peterson (first place), Lorrin Harrison (second place), A.D. Bayer (third place), Joe Parsons (fourth place), unknown (fifth place), Dexter Wook (sixth place), Hoppy Swartz (seventh place) and unknown (eighth place). Joe Parsons's board is an eleven-foot balsa with a mahogany deck. Note the change in surfboard design from previous contests.

On July 10, 1938, the West Coast Paddleboard Association held the contest under the auspices of the Del Mar Surf Club of Santa Monica. All types of boards could be used in the competition, which drew a crowd of 1,500 surf fans to the two-hour event. The turnout was said to have been the largest since the sport became popular. Pete Peterson emerged as the Pacific Coast Surfboard champion, beating out thirty-six contestants. Whitey Harrison of Dana Point came in second, while Adolph Bayer of Santa Monica came in third. Contest officials were Dr. A.H. Wilkes, president of the Del Mar Club; Ralph Saylin, secretary; Tom Blake; and Captain George Watkins of Santa Monica.

The first surf and paddleboard tournament on August 27, 1939, was also held in San Onofre. Sponsored by the San Clemente Chamber of Commerce, two thousand surfing fans from all over Southern California flocked to San Onofre to watch the races. Many had arrived the night before, building a huge bonfire from the railroad ties they had dragged along behind their cars, and partied all night. A dory had been anchored outside the surf line, and contestants paddled around the dory, giving their names as they passed.

Jim Bailey and his cocker spaniel, Rusty, were at the 1939 Pacific Coast Surfboard Championship. Some said the pair should have qualified for the mixed-couple surfing contest!

They then rode to shore, where their names where checked off again. The surfer who completed the fullest circles in an hour was the winner.

Sadly, the surf was not very big that day, and one of the scheduled events couldn't be held. However, Jim Bailey of Hermosa Beach pleased the crowd by riding his surfboard with his cocker spaniel, Rusty. Some said Jim and Rusty should have qualified for the mixed-couple surfing contest, but judges Merton Hackett and Dr. J.H. Hall nixed the idea. Instead, Pete Peterson and his wife, Arlene, garnered top honors in the mixed-couple contest. Peterson also led the field of eleven contestants in the paddleboard race. Merle Eyestone of Manhattan Beach came in second in the paddleboard event, while third-place honors went to Fred Kerwin of Hermosa Beach. In the mixed-couples race, James Kervin and Gladys Lavagnivo of Hermosa Beach ran second, while Vincent Lindberg and Eleanor Roach of San Onofre placed third. Rusty and Jim, however, received the most applause and inspired Pete Peterson to train his dog, a Scottie named Hughie, to become the finest surfing dog anyone had ever seen.

Over one hundred surfers, headed by Pete Peterson and Whitey Harrison, were back in San Onofre on July 14, 1940, to compete in the

Cliff Tucker from Palos Verdes was rated the most daring rider on the West Coast. One spectacular crash required thirty stitches and two hours to close the gap in Tucker's leg. It took three months to heal.

Southern California Surfing Championships. Peterson, a neat freak who never used any wax on the surface of his board for traction because he felt it violated the pristine look he so admired, had won the championship in 1936 and 1938 but bowed to Harrison in 1939. Dark horse of the meet was Cliff Tucker from Palos Verdes, who was rated the most daring rider on the West Coast. Tucker had suffered a painful injury in June when a loose board cut his ankle. A brother battle was also in the offing when Leroy and Don Grannis vied for honors under different colors. Leroy, the oldest at twenty-two, would compete for Palos Verdes, while brother Don, sixteen, would ride for Hermosa. (There is no mention of which brother won!) Other surfing "stars" included Hoppy Swartz, Adolph Bayer and Jimmy Reynolds of Palos Verdes; Jim Bailey, Jim Kerwin and Bill Edgar of Hermosa; and Erwin Lenkeit, Vincent Lindberg, Charles Butler and Joe Parsons.

It was Cliff Tucker who proved his surfing abilities were tops when he outgamed and outrode seventy-five surfing stars to win the Southern California Surfing Championship. Earlier in the day, when the wind was calm, Tucker

Pete Peterson won the 1941 Pacific Coast Surfboard Championship. He is seen here holding the perpetual cup. *From left to right*: Eddie McBride, Vincent Lindberg, Don Oakey, Dorian "Doc" Pascowitz, Jim Bailey, Lorrin "Whitey" Harrison, Tom Blake, Pete Peterson, Vincent VanBlom and Rusty Williams.

rode an ultra-light, hollow, 50-pound plywood board he had built with about five dollars' worth of materials. He called it his "Slanchwise"—an unorthodox surfboard that opponents said he wouldn't stand a chance with. Later, for the finals held in choppy conditions, Cliff used a heavier 120-pound spruce board, which wasn't affected by the wind and bumps. No one had ever thought of doing that before! After six hours of grueling competition, his switching boards led to victory over three opponents. The top ten contestants were: Cliff Tucker (Palos Verdes), Jim McGrew (Surfriders), Johnny Gates (Palos Verdes), Merle Eyestone (Manhattan Beach), Hoppy Swartz (Palos Verdes), Verne Lindbers (San Onofre), A.D. Beard (Surfriders), Ralph Kinner (San Onofre), Thayer Crispin (San Onofre) and Walt "Slim" Blom (San Onofre).

The last Pacific Coast Surfboard Championship was held in 1941. Unfortunately, we haven't been able to find much information about it other than the photos Doc Ball published in *California Surfriders*. It was Pete Peterson who won the event.

National Surfing and Paddleboard Contests
1938 and 1939

Surf contests were catching on, and two were held in Long Beach in 1938 and 1939. On November 14, 1938, the *Press-Telegram* noted:

DOZEN CLUBS IN SURF CONTESTS

Preston Peterson of Santa Monica and Miss Mary Ann Hawkins of the Del Mar Surfing Club yesterday were crowned national paddleboard champions in the first annual national surfing and paddleboard contest at Long Beach. Competing were 140 members of twelve organizations.

Lack of a heavy surf made necessary a postponement of competition in the surfriding events and the highly anticipated initial interclub clash for possession of the Dick Loynes perpetual team trophy until December 11.

Riding the small waves, John Olson of Long Beach won the open surfing event with James McGrew of Beverly Hills second and Denny Watson of Venice third. In the most thrilling event of the day, a five-man team from the Venice Surfriding Club nosed out the Manhattan Club at the finish of a relay event entered also by Long Beach and the Palos Verdes Surfriders.

On December 11, 1938, forty thousand onlookers watched sixty-five surfers compete in team and individual competitions in Long Beach. The Santa Ana Band led the participants, whose boards ranged in length from eleven to eighteen feet, to the edge of the surf between Rainbow and Silver Spray Piers, where the water temperature was fifty-two degrees. Newsreel, magazine and newspaper photographers were also there taking pictures of the event from all angles.

Press-Telegram, December 12, 1938
SURFRIDERS WATCHED BY BIG CROWD

Forty thousand onlookers yesterday watched one of the most thrilling aquatic demonstrations ever staged when nature provided thundering rollers for the third annual Mid-winter Swim coupled with the National Surfing Champions.

Postponed from a month ago, the National Surfing Championships provided the greatest action, with sixty-five surf riders participating. The Manhattan Surfing Club won the 44-inch silver perpetual team cup. The Venice Surfing Club placed second, Santa Monica third, Palos Verdes Surfriders Club fourth, and the Del Mar Club fifth. The open surfing championship was won by Arthur Horner of Venice, with Jim Kerwin of Manhattan Beach coming in second, and Don Campbell, also of Manhattan Beach, third. Medals were given to Chuck Allen, Palos Verdes, fourth place; Tom Ehlers, Manhattan Beach, fifth place; Kenneth Beck, Venice, sixth; and Bob Reinhard and John Lind of Long Beach, who placed seventh and eighth.

Press-Telegram, December 4, 1939
SURF EVENT IS WON BY HERMOSIANS

A three-man team representing the Hermosa Beach Surfing Club yesterday won the Dick Loynes perpetual trophy emblematic of the national surfing championship in an event in the fog-shrouded waters off Rainbow Pier.

Booming out of the fog blanket on the crests of curling breakers that saturated onlookers, the Hermosa Beach men nosed out the defending trophy holders of Manhattan Beach by 10 points. Venice Surfing Club was third and Long Beach, fourth. Gene Smith, member of the Hawaiian Surfing Club, which traveled here from the islands, competed alone against the teams after his two teammates A.C. Spohler and Jack May withdrew in the face of the unusual weather conditions. He finished fifth against the heavy odds.

Individual surfing honors went to Long Beach Surfing Club members John Olson, who finished first, Alvin Bixler, second, and Bob Reinhard, fourth. Gene Smith of Hawaii came in third.

PACIFIC COAST WATERMEN'S CHAMPIONSHIP AND WORLD WAR II

During the 1940s, Newport Beach continued to grow, and there was talk of changing the name. Since there were four principal villages at the time—Balboa, Newport, Balboa Island and Corona del Mar—all were hot contenders, but Balboa was the frontrunner. So heated was the debate that the matter was put to a vote in 1940: "Shall the name of the city of Newport Beach be changed from Newport Beach to Balboa?" The results? 1,014 against, 581 for. Newport Beach would remain Newport Beach!

Then came December 7, 1941, and the attack on Pearl Harbor. Immediately, the U.S. Coast Guard set up emergency centers up and down the coast, taking over the castle-like home built by William Collins on Collins Island and the Gillette home near the harbor entrance. On December 8, the U.S. Navy issued an ordinance requesting a complete, all-night blackout. This meant all illumination visible from the air or street was banned—blinds drawn and any outside lights turned off. Many complied by painting their windows black. Merchants announced that stores would close at 4:30 p.m. daily and open at 8:00 or 8:30 a.m. to take advantage of daylight hours.

All outdoor advertising, street lights, traffic lights and auto headlights were banned from dusk until dawn.

Throughout the Southland, there was fear of an eminent Japanese attack on the U.S. mainland. A naval defense zone was extended from the Los Angeles-Long Beach harbor down the coast to Newport Beach. All vessels entering the zone were warned that they did so at their own risk and that failing to comply would render them liable to attack. For six weeks, no boats were allowed to leave Newport Harbor. Finally, in late January 1942, restrictions were eased somewhat, but only those who had documentary proof of U.S. citizenship were allowed to sail.

With such strict rules in effect, surfers were putting their lives at risk by venturing into the sea. But they needn't worry for too long, because most would shortly be drafted into military service. Some, such as U.S. Marine Bob Silver, would be fortunate enough to be stationed at El Toro and have the opportunity (and nerve) to take up surfing. Silver felt that surfing personified the toughness of a U.S. Marine, calling it the world's most challenging sport, and likened it to skiing down a mountain slope that's going uphill.

The great surf at Corona del Mar has faded, but during huge south swells, surfing can be found on both sides of the Corona del Mar jetty. However, surfing on the harbor-mouth side can bring you a ticket or an arrest.

The Wedge began its birth with the demise of the 1921 Peninsula jetty. Today, it can produce waves up to thirty feet high.

There was one last Southern California surf contest held less than a month before the outbreak of World War II. Preston "Pete" Peterson continued to show his moxie by winning the first annual Pacific Coast Watermen's Championship in Santa Monica on November 11, 1941. Peterson, a Santa Monica lifeguard, led a field of thirteen contestants in a medley race that included one mile of swimming, a mile of paddleboarding and a mile of canoeing in the ocean between Santa Monica and Ocean Park piers. Peterson finished second in the swimming lap to Reggie Parton, also of Santa Monica, but soon took a 200-yard lead on the paddleboard lap, finishing 350 yards in front of Parton with a time of fifty-eight minutes, eight seconds.

Unfortunately, there would not be any other national surf contests until after the war. The Japanese attack on Pearl Harbor on December 7, 1941, plunged America into the battle that had been raging in Europe since 1939. Surfing would be different following the war, as would some of the early surf spots. Corona del Mar had already disappeared with the advent of the Corona jetty in 1936. In Long Beach, a breakwater would be completed in the harbor in the 1940s, and the U.S. Navy would come and make Terminal Island its home. After the war, the surfers who returned from battle would find that there were no more waves in Long Beach to ride—the breakwater had seen to that.

Though the great surf at Corona del Mar was no more, it continues when there is a south swell, appropriate for bodysurfing. During huge south swells, surfing can be found on both sides of the Corona del Mar jetty; however, surfing on the harbor-mouth side can bring you a ticket or an arrest. There is also the Wedge, located at the extreme west end of the Balboa Peninsula. It slowly began to gain momentum in 1927 with the completion of the west (Peninsula) jetty. The Wedge had begun with the building of the 1921 jetty, its birth pangs bringing about the demise of the first fifty yards of this first jetty. In 1936, with the completion of the revamped jetties, it sprang to life when a south swell of just the right size and direction hit the Peninsula jetty. It can produce waves up to thirty feet high and continues to lure surfers, bodysurfers and bodyboarders to this day.

Chapter 6

Surfboards

SURFBOARD EVOLUTION

At the turn of the twentieth century, there was a reawakening interest in surfing. As mentioned earlier, it was George Freeth who revived the art of riding a surfboard in a standing position in 1900. The boards in use at the time were generally six to eight feet in length and suitable only for bodyboarding. The shapes of the boards were random, as were the materials out of which they were shaped.

The ancient Hawaiians had used two types of boards: the alaia (thin) board and the olo (thick) board. Boards were made from koa, acacia, a balsa-like wood called wiliwili, breadfruit and other species. The desire to catch larger waves farther out from shore led to a revived interest in the boards used by ancient Hawaiians. The increased size meant you could paddle to these waves more easily than having to swim the smaller boards.

Freeth, discovering an ancient surfboard from pre-missionary days, persisted in trying to ride the breakers in a standing position on this antique find. However, the board, which was sixteen feet long and four inches thick, couldn't take the curve in the waves. Freeth came to realize that the old board he had been given was perfect for riding waves "in the green" before they broke but not while the wave was actually breaking. He finally calculated dimensions that worked in a breaking wave—eight feet long, twenty-four inches wide and four inches thick. This design was quickly adopted by the many Hawaiians who preferred to ride their surfboard standing up and while the wave was breaking.

An early 1890s–1900s Hawaiian "alaia" (short) board. This particular board stands eight feet, one inch and weighs thirty-six pounds.

About this time, redwood was being brought over from the mainland as a lightweight, bug-resistant building material. The size of many of the planks of redwood coming to the islands was around twenty-four inches wide, four inches thick and ten to twelve feet long. Surfboards started appearing with very similar dimensions to these same planks. The noses of the boards become more rounded, with square tails and a shape tapering from the nose to the tail. These boards tended to be flat on the top, were slightly bowed from nose to tail on the bottom and had rounded rails.

This redwood plank board was made by Duke Kahanamoku and Ron Drummond on the beach at Corona del Mar around 1928. It stands twelve feet tall and weighs fifty-five pounds.

What was an early twentieth-century surfboard like? Journalist Robert Burdette gives a delightful (though verbose) description in the February 26, 1910 *Los Angeles Times*:

> *A surfboard in appearance reminds you of nothing else so much as a coffin lid for a fat man. There the resemblance ends. For it has a birch bark canoe bolted to a rock bottom, for liveliness. The ark on Ararat wasn't half so firm as a surfboard is lively, restless, coquettish and full of strange and sudden surprises. It is the bucking bronco of all marine craft. It recognizes a tenderfoot the minute the doomed man lays hand on it. It will un-seahorse him when it is sound asleep, in ten inches of water. It will do things to him one day that it never thought of the day before, and will probably discard for something more sudden tomorrow.*

When the tender-fluke lays his manly figure on this malignant slab, like a boy swimming on a plank, he feels as safe as a circus rider on a barn door pad. He feels a scorn for this sort of so-called sport, as he lies there on his one-piece raft with an expression that his face cannot help but express. That lasts nearly half a minute. Then, at the first little swell, the sluggish plank, without the slightest effort, stands up on end but changes its mind and rolls over after hesitating a moment on one edge. It then crawls across the back of the submerged experimenter and starts alone for deep water under sealed orders.

As you have to wade out until you are too tired to walk any farther to find water deep enough to drown on Waikiki beach, the disaster is not so dangerous as it is unpleasant. But the man who comes to the surface has left that look of lofty scorn for the surfboard down at the bottom of the beautiful blue sea, hider of secrets, and he never recovers it. Not even after he has grown to be such a merman that the board is merely a part of himself, as the bronco is a mere detail of a cowboy's external system. During the days and weeks and maybe months of one's novitiate, the board is a tantalizing joy; a continuous performance of fascinating disappointments, a juggling marine fiend that speaks the word of promise to the unsteady feet and breaks it with a slapping splash that be heard all over the island.

But when one sees an Outrigger clubman on a surfboard, standing erect, his body with the grace of natural equilibrium, the stretched arm seeming to direct the invisible, the snowy crest of the surf tossing about his body the racing wave carrying him along like a dolphin mounted Arion, a creature with whom the seas tries to play; when sometimes a skillful rider stands on his head instead of his feet, just to show the staring malihini how easy it is—that is how it looks—then you comprehend the charm of riding; you admire the skill and grace which conceals its difficulties as the beautiful surf hides yet reveals the reef.

By 1920, the boards had changed. Originally, a few feet of foot-wide plank, pointed at one end, served as a surfboard. Often, like a kite suddenly deprived of a tail, the board would plunge to the bottom of the sea. When the pointed end of the board hit the sand, the rider felt like he had been hit across the midriff with a baseball bat. It was not uncommon to see many boards with the initials "R.R." painted on them. Like Teddy Roosevelt, those boards were "Rough Riders."

By 1922, there were two or three new makes of boards, according to the June 11, 1922 *Los Angeles Times*. They were all basically the same—light, buoyant and practically dive proof. One type of board was constructed like the wing of an airplane. It ranged in size from a small three-foot length for kids to a ten-foot length for the whole family to ride. The framework of light but durable wood with the bow, thicker than the midship and stern, formed the hull. The bow bent up slightly. Over the entire framework, several thicknesses of canvas were stitched on. Following this, the board was painted and varnished, leaving several air spaces inside, with the bow, with its larger body, acting as a buoy. On one side of the bow, a small hole was bored with a fitted rubber stopper. What little water seeped in was easily drained by pulling out the stopper and turning the board bow down. The board was very light. A man's board, about four and a half feet long, weighed only a few pounds. It was easy to hoist the board over the head and go out chest-deep in the water and wait for a breaker. It made no difference if the breaker had broken or was about to break, all one had to do was point the board toward shore and climb on—belly fashion or on the knees until the rider learned to stand up. The trailing legs and feet acted as a rudder or, by tilting the board up slightly on either side with the hands, as a way to steer it.

The innovations mentioned here in 1922 may have been picked up and refined by Tom Blake in his designs. In any case, it was Tom Blake who revolutionized the world of surfboard manufacturing with his hollow board design. Blake loved surfing and was delighted when he was able to restore old Hawaiian surfboards housed at the Bishop Museum in Hawaii. Since he could not take them out to Waikiki and ride or paddle them, he decided to build duplicates as an experiment. His object was to make a faster board using the ancient Hawaiian design.

During the 1920s, most surfboards weighed anywhere from 75 pounds to 150 pounds. A sixteen-foot olo board, which Tom was working to replicate, could weigh up to 200 pounds. Tom started with a solid, 250-pound piece of redwood that was sixteen feet long, two feet wide and four inches thick. On a whim, to try to lighten the slab, he hand drilled holes all the way through the "blank." Each hole removed a cylinder the same thickness as the slab, about four inches. He drilled hundreds of holes through the blank and then left it to season for a month. After seasoning the board, he covered the top and bottom with a thin layer of veneer to conceal and seal the holes. Finally, he shaped the blank to resemble one of Hawaiian chief Abner Paki's 1830s olo boards. As noted above, the final board was fifteen feet long, nineteen inches wide and four inches thick. It

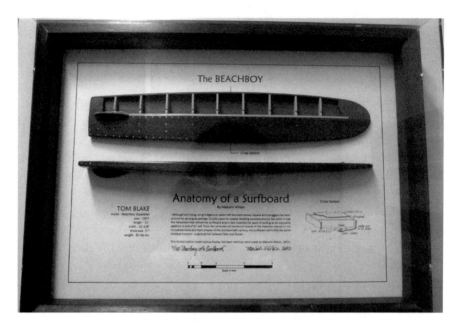

Anatomical view of Tom Blake's hollow board design.

weighed in at 110 pounds—still a very heavy board, but 140 pounds less than the slab he had begun with!

Tom's advantage in using this hollow board for paddling was not only its lighter weight but also its longer planing surface. A longer planing surface allowed the board to glide farther with each paddle stroke. Prior to his invention, participants in paddling contests used their regular surfboards, which were only ten to twelve feet long and much wider.

The evolution of the hollow board continued. It had originally been created in 1926 with the accidental use of drilled holes filled in to make air pockets. In 1929, Blake saw the implementation of full hollow chambers. The third step came in 1932 with Blake's use of the transversely braced hollow hull. By using ribs for strength, much like in an airplane wing, Tom brought the weight of the hollow boards down even further. The result, depending on the board's length, was a strong forty- to seventy-pound board. Blake's final refinement to the hollow board occurred in the late 1940s, when the board rails began to be rounded. With the rounded rail, water could move over and under the board with much less resistance.

It didn't take long for the hollow paddleboard to become an essential water rescue device. "The lifesaving possibilities are what will carry the hollow surfboard to future worldwide use," Blake predicted. He was partially right. As others took surfboard designs off in various directions, the hollow paddleboard was used mainly in lifesaving.

Besides his many other talents, Duke Kahanamoku also shaped surfboards. During one of his film shoots, he dropped down to Corona del Mar and fashioned a board on the beach for each of the Vultee brothers, Gerard and Art. It was the larger eleven-foot board that Gerard used in the 1928 Pacific Coast Surfboard contest. Though he did not consider hollow surfboards practical, Duke later incorporated some of Tom Blake's other ideas into his own surfboard designs.

The thirteen-foot-nine-inch plywood paddleboard, shown in the center, was built by Elsworth Booth in 1935 and weighs fifty-eight pounds. It was used by Newport Beach lifeguards in the 1930s and '40s.

In 1927, two Orange County surfers who were members of the Corona del Mar surfing crowd decided to try their hand at making surfboards. When Delbert "Bud" Higgins decided to build his own board in 1927, Duke Kahanamoku suggested that an eleven-foot board was too large for his body size, so Higgins and his friend Gene Belshe decided to make two scaled-down ten-foot boards. For forty dollars, they found they could buy a solid plank of kiln-dried redwood that was twenty feet long, two feet wide and three inches thick. They cut the plank in half and shaped two boards with a block plane and drawknife. After three months, the completed boards weighed 135 pounds each, almost too heavy to carry, but the young men still believed the "classic" redwood boards were best! At the same time, others, such as Keller Watson, began experimenting with redwood-balsa wood combinations.

Top: A 1920s board featuring the flying "V." Nine feet, four inches long and weighing seventy-six pounds, it is one of two boards created by Duke Kahanamoku for brothers Gerard and Art Vultee on the sand in Corona del Mar before the east (Corona) jetty was extended.

Middle: Kahanamoku carved his name above the flying "V" on this board at the Surfing Heritage Museum.

Bottom: A sign detailing the history of the board.

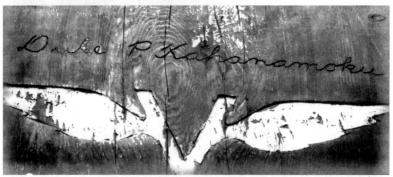

9'4" SOLID REDWOOD BY DUKE KAHANAMOKU C.1920'S. THIS SURFBOARD IS THOUGHT TO BE ONE OF TWO SHAPED BY DUKE KAHANAMOKU FOR THE VULTEE BROTHERS IN THE LATE 1920'S. ORIGINALLY MUCH LONGER, THE BOARD WAS RESHAPED BY JOE QUIGG IN 1961. THE ORIGINAL "FLYING V" WAS RE-CARVED AND THE BOARD REFINISHED IN 1989 AS A MEMORIAL TO THE VULTEES WHO WERE EARLY PIONEERS OF SURFING IN CORONA DEL MAR.
(PRIVATE COLLECTION)

Above, left: The front of the second board crafted by Duke Kahanamoku. This board was used in the 1928 Pacific Coast Surfboard Contest by Gerard Vultee.

Above, right: The front of the second Vultee board has been modified in recent years—the "V" and the area around it carved out.

Below: The back of the second Vultee board shaped in Corona de Mar by Duke Kahanamoku for the Vultee brothers.

With many young surfers going off to war, the idyllic days of surfing were soon to come to an end. But surfers were still looking, thinking and planning on ways to improve the boards used in their beloved sport once they returned home. In a way, the war had an influence on surfing. As a naval power, the United States' need for aquatic products increased. Rubber, fiberglass, Styrofoam and other innovations appeared, and the imaginations of these beach boys helped incorporate these new advances into the surfing industry we have today.

HOW TO RIDE A SURFBOARD

Do you want to know how to ride a surfboard? Why not let some famous names be your guide? In his 1907 book *Learning Hawaiian Surfing: A Royal Sport at Waikiki Beach, Honolulu,* Jack London described how to surf. (Remember, this was in the days when photography and motion pictures were rare, and words alone had to suffice to describe how to do something).

Get out on a flat board, six feet long, two feet wide, and roughly oval in shape. Lie down upon it like a small boy on a coaster and paddle with your hands out to deep water, where the waves begin to crest. Lie out there quietly on the board. Sea after sea breaks before, behind, and under and over you, and rushes in to shore, leaving you behind. When a wave crests, it gets steeper. Imagine yourself, on your board, on the face of that steep slope. If it stood still, you would slide down just as a boy slides down a hill on his coaster. "But," you object, "the wave doesn't stand still." Very true, but the water composing the wave stands still, and there you have the secret. If ever you start sliding down the face of that wave, you'll keep on sliding, and you'll never reach the bottom. Please don't laugh. The face of that wave may be only six feet, yet you can slide down it a quarter of a mile, or half a mile, and not reach the bottom. For since a wave is only a communicated agitation or impetus, and since the water that composes a wave is changing every instant, new water is rising into the wave as fast as the wave travels. You slide down this new water and yet remain in your old position on the wave, sliding down the still newer water that is rising and forming the wave. You slide precisely as fast as the wave travels. If it travels fifteen miles an hour, you slide fifteen miles an hour. Between you and shore stretches a quarter of mile of water. As the wave travels, this water obligingly heaps itself into the wave, gravity does the rest, and down you go, sliding the whole length of it. If you still cherish the notion, while sliding, that the water is moving with you, thrust your arms into it and attempt to paddle; you will find that you have to be remarkably quick to get a stroke, for that water is dropping astern just as fast as you are rushing ahead.

The water in the over toppling crest does move forward, as you will speedily realize if you are slapped in the face by it, or if you are caught under it and are pounded by one mighty blow down under the surface panting and gasping for half a minute. The water in the top of a wave rests upon the water in the bottom of the wave. But when the bottom of the wave strikes the land, it stops, while the top goes on. It no longer has the bottom of the wave to hold it up. Where was solid water beneath it is now air, and for the first time, it feels the grip of gravity, and down it falls, at the same time being torn asunder from the lagging bottom of the wave and flung forward. And it is because of this that riding a surf-board is something more than a mere placid sliding down a hill. In truth, one is caught up and hurled shoreward as by some Titan's hand.

The surfboards George Freeth used to teach others to surf were of redwood, weighed about forty pounds and incorporated his successful formula (eight feet long, twenty-four inches wide and two inches thick). He told his students that once they left the beach, they were to carry the board until they couldn't touch bottom, hold the board off to one side and then head into the breakers. Otherwise, the breaker could catch the board and send the novice surfer sprawling. The second thing they had to do was lie flat on the board with their feet hooking just over the end and paddle with their arms as if they were oars. At the same time, the beginner was to balance the board by pressing down with the chest on whichever side the board was to be directed. Thirdly, they were to start paddling about twenty feet from the breaker and to keep paddling until they fully caught the wave. They were then to slide backward off the board until the end of it struck between the knees and hips. This was to remove the weight from the front of the board to keep it from running into the sand. As the board rode over the breakers and up to the beach, the surfer was to use his feet as a rudder to steer, and as he was carried into shore, he was to hold the board with both hands.

Freeth also provided safety tips. The rider must never get between the breaker and the board, or he could be hit by the heavy board. The rider also had to paddle until he was fully up to the breaker. Above all things, the rider had to remember not to slide off the board too far when taking the wave—

that is, the foot of the board should touch the legs of the rider between the hips and the knees, otherwise the board might strike the surfer in the body. The last thing and most important to remember was to never to let go of the board.

Here's what Duke Kahanamoku had to say about the sport almost twenty years later in the June 19, 1927 issue of the *Los Angeles Times*:

DUKE KAHANAMOKU EXPLAINS TECHNIQUE OF SUCCESSFULLY RIDING SKIDDING SURFBOARD

Riding a giant breaker at express-train speed is perhaps the most invigorating and thrilling sport in the world. It combines thrills with endurance, skill and strength. I know of no other pastime which supplies such a variety of sensations nor which assists more in promoting sound health, cast-iron muscles and perfect mind coordination.

Let us take for granted that you've never ridden a surfboard in your life. That will give me some definite object at which to shoot, and I will be certain not to overlook anything.

A surfboard is a flat plank, ten, twelve, or fourteen feet long, planed so it comes to a point at one end. Good seasoned redwood is the best material. It is neither too light nor too heavy and is slow to absorb water.

The length of the board depends largely upon one's own weight and preference. The one I am using is twelve feet long. I consider this the correct size for a man of my build—204 pounds. The thickness of the board should be about three inches and the width about two feet. The back part of the board, the corners, should be slightly rounded to avoid hard edges.

Before being put into the water, it is imperative that it be given at least four coats of Valspar or some other reliable waterproof varnish. I do not consider hollow surfboards practical, although many prefer them to the solid wooden ones.

With the board made—or purchased, as the case may be—we are ready for our first lesson. The manner of carrying the board is largely a matter of personal preference. When out of the water, I prefer to carry it with the center of the board resting in the crotch of my left arm and the hand steadying it at the top.

Arriving at the water's edge, hold the board upright in front of you—just off the ground—with one hand grasping each side at the center place. Place the board flat in the water, lie on it stomach down, feet close together, and extend one arm on each side to paddle out.

Considerable difficulty may be experienced in this first operation. If the sea is running high, one is certain to have several upsets before reaching the breaker line. When you see a big breaker approaching, it is simpler to meet it if one slides into the water at the back of the board and lifts the rear of it high enough so that the nose dips into the water. In this manner the wave will wash over it. Then, when the breaker has passed, climb back and continue to paddle.

Once outside the breaker line, turn the board shoreward and straddle it in the center, treading water with your feet. This will give you an opportunity to rest a moment. When you spot a big breaker, lie upon your stomach again, legs together, and paddle toward it with your hands. It is possible to steer the board by shifting the position of one's feet or body.

When you are on top of the wave, the most difficult part of the entire operation is encountered—that of crawling to a standing position without upsetting. The movements are as follows:

First, with a quick motion, jump from your flat position to your hands and knees. Second, with all the speed possible, get to one's feet. By this time, you are probably traveling thirty-five miles an hour, and the utmost caution must be exercised that you do not upset.

One should stand close to the rear of the board with the leg positioned much the same as that of a prizefighter about to deliver a blow. The right foot should be on the right side of the board and a little forward, while the left foot should favor the left side about eighteen inches to the rear of the right foot. In this way, you are perfectly braced. Do not, under any circumstances, keep your feet together. You will be caught off balance, and the result will be disastrous.

The best location to ride surf is, of course, where the waves are largest and where they break far out at sea. An eighth of a mile is considered a fair distance. During the filming of Paramount's Old Ironsides among the Channel Islands of the Pacific, we discovered several spots where the surf extended more than a mile into the ocean. The longest surf I know is at the northwest end of the Hawaiian Islands—off the island of Niihau. Here the breakers run a good five miles at lightning speed.

If you are proficient, you will make a good surfboard rider. Women, as a rule, make better surfboard artists than men. In my experience as an instructor, this has proven to be true on almost every occasion. While for actual strength and endurance, men are far superior, women, it seems, have a better sense of balance.

Among the people I have assisted in learning the past two years are such notables as Esther Ralston, Wallace Beery, George Bancroft, Florence Vidor and Bebe Daniels. Miss Daniels, by the way, learned more rapidly than any other pupil I have ever encountered. Her sense of balance is perfect.

After one becomes more accustomed to the surfboard and the tumbles grow fewer, one can experiment in trick riding—riding backwards, standing on your hands, riding with someone perched on your shoulders. There is always some new idea.

Chapter 7

Other Ways to Ride the Surf

Inlanders coming to Newport Beach wanted to have fun. Perhaps the biggest holiday of the year was the Fourth of July, when it seemed you could blow up the whole town if you could get enough gunpowder. The people on Balboa shot skyrockets across the bay at Balboa Island, and the folk on Balboa Island shot skyrockets across the bay at the people in Balboa. People shot Roman candles at each other across the street. Somehow, no one ended up killed or severely injured. But that was Newport Beach—a place in which residents of the present town wouldn't want to be caught dead in!

Besides drinking, gambling and dancing, there was the aquatic sports industry, which men such as Balboa postmaster Fred Beckwith promoted. Beckwith had learned canoeing from an Indian in his old home in Michigan and later built the first canoe used on local waters, according to the April 11, 1909 *Los Angeles Times*. He organized the Balboa Canoe Club and purchased a carload of canoes for local use. In 1908, Beckwith met up with New Yorker William Jones, who entertained crowds by shooting the Newport Beach breakers in a canoe. Always on the lookout for novel ways to attract a crowd, Beckwith instituted a number of aquatic activities to entertain visitors, including the "sport" of canoe tilting, a featured event at one of the nation's first surf contests, held in Newport Beach's Corona del Mar in 1928. In a two-man canoe, one person paddled while the other carried a long pole fitted on the end with a pad about the size of a football. With this weapon, he tried to overthrow his opponent, similarly armed, from the other canoe.

Aquatic activities were the lifeblood of early Newport Beach, and many water sports, such as aquaboarding and bodysurfing, originated here. Every Fourth of July before World War I, the Balboa Water Show Association put on a program

The Balboa Canoe Club was started by Balboa postmaster Fred Beckwith around 1908. Canoeing was a popular way to tour Newport Bay.

that included a swimming race, a tug-of-war between rowboats and a sailboat and canoe and motorboat races. Also included was an exhibition of surfboard riding. However, it wasn't quite the "surfing" we think of today. In 1916, for instance, Fred Brown, Harold Knight, Homer Church and William Collins entertained the hordes by standing on their heads, as well as doing other daring stunts, while riding their surfboards behind speedboats. It was promoters like Beckwith who realized that bay sports were terrific moneymakers if you only knew how to use and advertise them properly.

CANOE SURFING

It was in 1908, at a water pageant at Balboa, that surf canoeing hit the Southern California shores. Originally, rowboats were the vessel of choice,

but getting a rowboat through the surf was difficult. The boat had too much of a bottom, making it more work than sport.

Newport promoter Fred Beckwith suggested using a small canoe, six or seven feet long and not more than two feet across in the center. These canoes, which he called "surf canoes," were also light enough for one man, woman or child to handle in the water and could easily be carried by two ordinary persons—or one ambitious man. They proved to be an instant success.

Surf canoeing had to be done at the right time. High tide was the worst time, so before renting a canoe, it was important to take a look at the surf. It was advised to leave the sport alone if the tide was running high, unless you liked such stunts as going over Niagara Falls in a barrel or jumping out of an airplane with a silk parasol for a parachute. Low tide was the preferred choice.

There were two ways of getting a canoe through the breakers. One was by pushing it through, and the other was paddling. In either case, it was important to have the bow of the canoe pointed toward the breaker. When the wave came in, the canoe rider had to lean with his weight on the stern. This lifted the point

Canoe and board surfing in the harbor entrance, 1930s.

Camping and homemade outrigger canoes on the beach at Corona del Mar, 1930s.

of the canoe out of the water and sort of skipped the boat over the wave. It was imperative that a canoe avoid going over a breaker broadsides—unless the occupant relished gulping seawater, gasping for air and seeing stars.

Once beyond the breakers, the surf canoer would have a delightful time paddling and bouncing on the swells until he was so tired he longed for shore. Returning to shore, however, one had to face the problem of shooting the breakers. There was a technique in getting the canoe back to dry land. It was important to shift to the middle of the boat, leaving more of the boat for the breakers to get hold of. Then all one had to do was paddle toward shore, making sure that the boat was at right angles to the breakers. If the canoer were dumped into the water, he would need to dive back of the breaker to avoid having the canoe hit him on the head.

Cashing in on the popularity of surf canoeing and surfing, Victor K. Hart and T. Bennett Shutt opened a factory in Long Beach. In February 1921, *Long Beach Press* reporters visited their workshop and found a dozen canoes and twenty surfboards in various stages of construction. The surfboards were of Hart and Shutt's own design and were lighter and different in shape than the Hawaiian island boards (too bad the reporters didn't describe them in more detail!). What of their canoes? Could one of them have been purchased by the mysterious "Two O'clock Kid."

During the waning days of Prohibition, all kinds of tales were woven around the mysterious "Two O'clock Kid." Nobody—not even other whisky smugglers—seemed to know his real name. If the Kid couldn't come in at 2:00 a.m., he didn't come in at all until the next morning, and then at the same hour. All anyone knew for certain was that he was an expert at maneuvering his craft through the surf and riding the breakers up to the sand. Many believed he perfected his skills by practicing canoeing during the day while also enjoying the sun, surf and girls along the beach. Could the Kid have been famed canoe surfer Ron Drummond? Drummond, born in 1907, would have been the right age. The six-foot-six swimmer, surfer, bodysurfer and canoer was also a UCLA track star who wanted to be an adventurer like his dad. Smuggling whiskey by canoe would have certainly qualified. To this day, nobody knows why the Two O'clock Kid insisted on smuggling his illicit brew in at two o'clock in the morning, and nobody ever learned his real name. "Canoe" Drummond, known up and down the Southern California coast for his canoeing expertise, would have definitely had the skills to fit the bill. Unfortunately, he died in 1996 and isn't around to shed any light on this mystery.

BODYSURFING

During the late 1920s and early 1930s, Balboa, on the peninsula, and the eight-hundred-foot Corona del Mar jetty became great Meccas for bodysurfing. It was here in Newport Beach that bodysurfing originated, according to the September 29, 1932 edition of the *Costa Mesa Herald*. It was in 1919 that Ludy Langer, who in the 1920 Olympics would win a silver medal in the 400-meter freestyle swimming event, showed that breakers could be ridden without a board. The general bodyboard in use at the time was about four feet long, a foot and a half across and about one inch thick. It was sometimes curved up at the nose to give the breakers something to catch a hold of, but it later proved to be more ornamental than useful. But Langer's novel approach to a wave meant that that no board was needed. It was simple, really; instead of putting both his hands out straight when riding the wave, he extended his arms by his side, banking his hands at his hips. This kept his head out of the water and allowed him to breathe at all times.

There was something about the contour of the bottom that made for great surf at the Balboa Pier. According to Robert Gardner, when you took off, you glanced to your right, and if you saw water running down the floor of the pier, you knew you had a big wave. Bodysurfing was very primitive in these pre–swim fin days. Because you couldn't generate enough speed to go left or right on the wave, you went straight—"over the falls." Without fins, you prayed you had caught the last wave of the set. Otherwise, you got yourself beaten to death until the set was over.

The *Costa Mesa Herald* described bodysurfing as "floating along with the breakers, without taking strokes as in swimming and without any board or other mechanical aid." Spectators, unfamiliar with this new sport of surf riding, were told by those in the know that there were two different varieties of bodysurfing. In one, the arms were extended beachward while the rider moved along in the lather of a wave. The second and more spectacular way of bodysurfing required the rider to clamp the arms against the sides, push the shoulders forward and

An aerial view of Balboa Pier, 1933. The Balboa Pier was a popular spot for bodysurfing in the days before the Newport Harbor was completed.

stick the head down and to ride the wave face down. Those who used this method became experts at "taking the drop" with a crashing breaker and riding part and parcel with it until it cast itself upon the sand.

In 1931, Ron Drummond, who was also an avid canoe surfer, would publish the first book on bodysurfing, *The Art of Wave Riding*. The small twenty-six-page booklet was one of the first books ever published about surfing. In his introduction, Drummond wrote, "To spend a day in the sand developing a beautiful tan is pleasant, but the real pleasure of a trip to the beach is derived from playing in the breakers"—something bodyboarders definitely enjoyed at Corona del Mar and the Balboa Pier and continue to relish today at one of the most famous bodysurfing spots in the world, Newport Beach's the Wedge.

Aquaplaning

Ever hear of aquaplaning? It was the most popular aquatic sport at Balboa thanks mainly to Vance Vieth. It was Vieth, a swimming instructor at the Los Angeles Athletic Club, who introduced the sport at Balboa in August 1916. The sport took a brief hiatus with America's deeper involvement in World War I, but following the war, Vieth was determined to revive the new sport. To do so, Vance was at Balboa every weekend in 1919 providing information and instruction on this latest aquatic fad.

In July 1919, Vieth showed a lot of moxie by being dragged through the water and air at the rate of forty miles an hour. This courageous feat set the fastest aquaplane record in Southern California. Newport Bay was perfect for the sport because it was calm and had little wave action. Vieth advised his students to stay away from the open ocean. Aquaplaning in the open ocean was only for the pros, he stated, since there were too many swells in which beginners could get tangled up.

Generally speaking, the "sport" of aquaplaning could be defined as standing on a board at the end of a rope and being dragged through the water by a motorboat at about fifteen miles an hour or better. Now does it sound familiar? Yes! Water skiing. Now it's done on one or two skis, but back in the beginning, it was done on boards of various sizes. The general rule was the bigger the board the safer and slower the sport. The largest boards were roughly four feet across and five feet long. The best board for single riding was generally one foot across and four feet long. The rope used had to be long enough to get the aquaboard rider well away from the propeller—fifteen feet was a good length. A ride started

The answer
to thirst
after play

Drink

Coca-Cola

Delicious and Refreshing

5¢

Aquaplaning was so popular that Coca Cola used the new sport in its ads.

with the motorboat slowly gaining speed and the rider lying down flat on the board. As the boat gathered speed, the rider would rise on one knee and grab the rope on the front of the board. Then the aquaboarder would stand up and lean back, holding onto the rope for dear life.

The nose of the board had to be kept elevated and out of the water. This meant standing well back on the board. If the nose did get into the water, the whole board would somersault and toss the rider into the motorboat or the propeller—or just in front of the board, where it would most likely hit him.

The important point about aquaplaning was to always fall sideways or backward and never jump in front of the board. Once free of the board, all the rider had to do was come to the surface of the water and paddle around until the motorboat came back. But a rider left in front of the board could get tangled up with the rope and possibly drown.

The hardest part of aquaplaning was making the turns. When the motorboat turned and swept the board around a curve, the rider had to lean toward the center of the curve and bank the board up on the outside all the way. It was easy to lean too far and end up in the bay.

If things got too dull, the rider could drop the ropes and try to balance himself without any assistance. Another way to get thrills was to sway sideways on the board, making it skip from side to side.

Auto Shoes

In the summer of 1915, riding waves on rubber "surf" boards became the latest Southern California beach fad. Anyone who grew up in the age when car tires had inner tubes probably at one time or another tackled the surf with an inner tube from dad's old car tires. But back in the day, when automobiles themselves were still somewhat of a fad, riding on inflated tire tubes seemed a novel idea.

Maybe it was just an advertisement for Firestone tires when A.T. Smith, manager of the Venice Firestone tire branch, invited Freddy Welsh, lightweight boxing champion of the world, to join him at the beach for a new experience.

The tubes were inflated with air, and for about an hour, the swimmers on their Firestone tubes entertained the crowds with numerous stunts on the water. Though it was difficult for the average swimmer to handle a surfboard, riding on an inner tube filled with air was as safe as you could get—except that you had to be careful of the air spigot that stuck out of the tube! Contact with the spigot while riding a wave was painful and could even put out an eye.

Following the demonstration, beachgoers flocked to their closest tire agency to pick up an old tube and enjoy the surf.

Surf Sled

In May 1932, Bill Wheeler, who worked for the *Los Angeles Times* art department, applied for a patent for his "Olympic Safety Surf Sled." After witnessing many accidents to those riding flat surfboards, Wheeler began to experiment with new designs. For over a year, you'd find him at the beach every Sunday studying different surfboard models. Wheeler soon found that all surfboards had the one bad fault of "nosediving."

Wheeler's design included a reinforced airtight compartment under the front end, which he claimed would prevent diving, even in the roughest water. Now anyone who could drag Wheeler's surf sled out over the water by its rope handles could enjoy all the thrills experienced by flat-board surfers.

The airtight compartments were made in two shapes; one had a bulbous bow and was tapered toward the rear, while the other tapered from the front end and was square at the rear. This second shape was known as the "hook" type, as it hooked the wave, so to speak, when the water rushed under the sled and started it speeding to shore. A stabilizer, or rudder, was attached to the underside of the sled at the rear, preventing "shimmying" or tipping over when coming in contact with cross currents. Wooden "monkey grip" handles were affixed to the top front sides, giving the rider a firm grip while plowing through the water. Without this, it was impossible at times to cling to the sled when traveling at a high rate of speed.

Wheeler's first models were made of kiln-dried, tongue-and-groove California redwood pieces sealed together with waterproof glue. One-inch strips of hardwood spleens inserted in both ends of the board prevented warping. After

The birth of the bodyboard—the surf sled.

the sleds were assembled, their metal tanks were enameled, and the boards were treated, first with oil, then stained and varnished. When finished, the sleds weighed eight to ten pounds, in accordance with their length and width.

PILLOWCASE SURFING

It was a novelty that originated in Long Beach in 1939 and was gaining new followers every day. Some actually believed it threatened to take the limelight enjoyed by the time-honored South Seas surfboard. Proponents stressed that if worst came to worst, it was better to be banged on the head by a bundle of air than a heavy surfboard—at least that's what they hoped you'd believe.

How did it begin? Lifeguards said that maybe somebody washed a pillowcase in the surf and accidentally discovered that a wet, inflated pillowcase made a dandy float.

Mothers didn't need to fear a raid on their bedding, for ordinary pillowcases were too small for surfing purposes. A bag three times as large and made of muslin was best, according to expert "pillowcasers." The bag had to be soaked with water, scooped full of air (running along the beach and catching the breeze in it was the favored method) and doused, open end down, until the rider had twisted the open end closed. The bag then was ready for use. Experts would carry their inflated pillowcases overhead while wading out to meet a breaker. When a big wave came, the pillowcase surfer would launch the pillowcases, leap aboard and sail shoreward in a salty lather.

There was only one hitch in pillowcase riding, lifeguards said. If a pillowcaser couldn't swim, he'd better stay in shallow water. When a big breaker yanked an inflated pillowcase from a non-swimmer in deep water, lifeguards had to make a rescue.

Epilogue

D espite the loss of Corona del Mar as a surfing Mecca in 1936, even today, given the right conditions, Corona can awaken and remind us all of the beautiful wave machine it once was. But surfing continues in Newport Beach. The Wedge has replaced Corona as the crown jewel of Newport Beach surfing, having risen to prominence with the harbor jetty changes that ended Corona del Mar's renown.

 The carefree days of surfing ended when regulations regarding board riding were instituted. In July 1960, the Newport Beach City Council defined four areas of surfing and adopted an ordinance restricting surfing area and hours:

> *Area 1: Near the mouth of the Santa Ana River, from Olive St. to the westerly city limits, commonly known as River Jetties. No restrictions as to surfing hours.*

> *Area 2: Between 36th St. and 42nd St. in West Newport. Surfing permitted only between 7:30 a.m. and noon, and limited to a designated two-block area, marked with signs. The signs to be moved at least once each week.*

> *Area 3: Near Newport Pier, from 19th St. to 20 feet southeast of the pier. This includes the area known to surfers as "Blackie's." No restrictions as to surfing hours.*

> *Area 4: At the main Corona del Mar beach, a 180 foot strip beginning 20 feet from the east jetty. Surfing is permitted only from 6:00 a.m. to*

The Corona del Mar jetty, 1934.

The jetty at Corona del Mar today—a rare day breaking.

noon, Monday through Friday, and 6:00 a.m. to 10:00 a.m. Saturdays, Sundays and holidays.

Later, in 1966, a yellow flag with a black ball in its center would be used to call surfers out of the water.

Surfers in the 1960s had to overcome the "surf bum" image that became a stereotype following surf movies such as *Gidget* and the "Beach Party" Frankie Avalon and Annette Funicello films of that decade. In 1961, for instance, Hermosa Beach wouldn't allow "surf bums" to participate in its July 29–30 surfing contest unless they submitted certificates from their high schools indicating they had grades high enough to qualify for school athletics. In addition, only entrants having adult sponsors and those that showed they were "self-policed" would be allowed to enter. The regulations, according to Mayor John deGroot, were to upgrade the qualifications for surfers and to provide a "healthy situation" for youngsters who took part in the popular sport. However, following up on these "rules" took too much of the city's time, and it was decided that individual surfing would be replaced by team competition, limiting the number of teams to six, with each team having four contestants and two alternates. In addition, each participant had to be able to prove satisfactory scholarship and citizenship records from the recent school year.

Following this trend, Newport Beach in 1966 instituted a three-dollar city license fee in the form of a decal placed on the surfboard. It seemed that licensing surfboards would become a state law, with the state of California collecting the money, but a state surfboard-licensing bill also introduced in 1966 died in committee. The Newport ordinance was repealed in December 1969. Councilmen said the repeal was a reward for surfers who, in recent years, had "improved their image" by observing regulations and respecting the rights of other water users. About two thousand boards were licensed under the old law.

Today, surfers still enjoy the waves of Newport Beach even though the breakers have changed since the completion of the harbor entrance. We have surf spots known as River Jetties (around the Santa Ana River mouth), the Numbered Streets (such as Twenty-eighth and Fifty-sixth), Blackie's (the area from the west side of the Newport Pier to the Twenty-eighth Street jetty), the Point (around Nineteenth Street), the Schoolyards (the area in front of Newport Elementary School) and, of course, the Wedge (the west side of the Peninsula jetty). Skimboarding has also entered the surfing scene, with the best conditions found at the Balboa Pier.

A view of Newport Harbor jetties today.

One thing that hasn't changed, however, is the love a surfer has of the sea. To paraphrase Jack London:

> *If a man is born a surfer and has gone to the school of the sea, never in all his life can he get away from the sea again. The savor of the salt never stales. The surfer never grows so old that he does not care to go back for one more wrestling bout with the wave. The salt of it is in his bones as well as his nostrils, and the sea will call to him until he dies.*

Or, as co-author Paul Burnett puts it, "You can always take a surfer out of the salt water, but you can never take the salt water out of a surfer."

Newport Bay & Surfing Timeline

1824–25   Floods create Balboa Peninsula and sandbars that would become islands.

1861   First published survey of Newport Bay.

1870   Bay acquires name "Newport" with arrival of ship *Vaquero*.

1888   McFadden builds a 1,300-foot wharf on the ocean.

1891   Steam railway links Newport with Santa Ana.

1892   James McFadden purchases the major part of the Balboa Peninsula (from Fortieth Street to Ninth Street) for a dollar an acre, lays out a town site near the wharf and begins to sell land.

1896   James Irvine fills in sandspits to create Balboa, Lido and Harbor Islands in the bay.

1902	Newport town site sold to developer William Collins.
1905	*Sport of surfing revived in Hawaii with the creation of the informal Hui Nalu (Club of the Waves).*
	Pacific Electric railway extended to Newport.
	George Hart purchases Corona del Mar from James Irvine.
1906 (July)	Pacific Electric rail line extended to Balboa.
	Balboa Pavilion and Balboa Pier open.
1906 (September)	City of Newport Beach incorporated.
1907	*George Freeth surfs Corona del Mar.*
	Newbert Protection District formed to control the Santa Ana River.
	Santa Ana River channel is established to divert water into Newport Bay.
1908	*Canoes first used to ride Corona waves.*
1909	*Felix Modjeski (grandson of Madame Modjeska) inherits grandmother's home on Bay Island and brings his surfboard with him.*
1911 (April)	South Coast Yacht Club establishes "Station A" at Balboa Peninsula.
1912	*Duke Kahanamoku reported to have surfed Corona del Mar, according to Art Vultee.*

1914 (March)	Ocean channel of Newport Bay choked by silt from heavy rains.
1914 (September)	*Duke Kahanamoku surfs Corona del Mar, according to press reports of the time.*
1915 (February)	The F.D. Cornell Company trades land in Riverside County to Corona del Mar founder George Hart.
1915–1916	Major flooding of the Santa Ana River.
1916 (September 25)	The citizens of Newport Beach approve a $125,000 bond to build one jetty off the Balboa Peninsula.
1916	Balboa joins Newport Beach.
1917	*Corona del Mar surfer Boyd Everett brings back surfboard from Hawaii.*
1917 (September)	Peninsula (West) jetty construction begins. *Surfing demonstrations part of celebration.*
1919	*The sport of bodyboarding originates in Newport Beach when Ludy Langer shows that breakers can be ridden without a board.*
1919 (June)	Bond passed to lengthen the Peninsula jetty two hundred to four hundred feet.
1920 (December)	New outlet for the Santa Ana River completed. It no longer drains directly into Newport Bay.

1921	Peninsula jetty extension completed.
1922	Joe Beek, the first harbor master, has a bell buoy placed one hundred feet south of the end of the Peninsula jetty. It was the first lighted marker in the harbor.
	William Sparr purchases Corona del Mar from the F.D. Cornell Company.
1922 (August)	*Duke Kahanamoku again surfs Corona del Mar.*
1923	Construction flaws in jetty become obvious. *The surfing area known as the "Wedge" begins its birth.*
1923 (April)	Corona del Mar annexed to Newport Beach.
1923 (December)	Lighthouse and lifeguard service inaugurated.
1924	Construction of Sparr Bathhouse (home of the Corona del Mar Surf Club) begins.
1925 (March 21)	Pacific Coast Highway between Long Beach and Newport Beach opens.
1925 (June)	*Duke Kahanamoku rescues shipwreck victims.*
1926 (May)	Fun zone on Balboa Peninsula opens.
1926 (July)	William Sparr puts all his holdings of Corona del Mar's water frontage, bluff lots and 350 lots on top of Corona del Mar, up for sale.

1926 (October 9)	Pacific Coast Highway between Newport Beach and Laguna Beach opens.
1927 (February)	East jetty (Corona) construction and extension of Peninsula jetty bond passed. *The surfing area known as the "Wedge" continues to form.*
1928 (Spring)	Dredging of Newport Bay for Transpacific and International Star Yacht Races.
1928 (May)	Transpacific Yacht Race originates in Newport.
1928 (August)	*First Pacific Coast Surfboard Competition and International Star yacht race held in Newport Bay and Corona del Mar.*
1929 (September)	*Second Pacific Coast Surfboard Competition at Corona del Mar.*
1931 (April)	Bal Week begins in Balboa on the Balboa Peninsula.
1932 (September)	*Third Pacific Coast Surfboard Competition at Corona del Mar.*
1933 (March)	Large earthquake centered off Newport.
1933 (December)	Funds okayed to extend jetties.
1936 (May)	Extended jetties complete. *Corona del Mar surfing ends.*
1939 (September)	Hurricane hits coast. *Surfers John Lugo and Ralph Dawson rescue shipwrecked fishermen.*
1940	Jetties repaired and new piers built at Balboa and Newport as a result of the hurricane.

Bibliography

"All Clear at Newport Beach: Anglers Must Show Proof of Citizenship in Order to Sail." *Los Angeles Times*, January 22, 1942, p.15.

Almond, Elliott. "Long May They Wave After All These Years; Surfing Still Holds Charm for Keller Watson, Lorrin Harrison." *Los Angeles Times*, July 13, 1989, p.1.

"Among Builders and Architects: On Newport Bay." *Los Angeles Times*, August 13, 1905, p.V-22.

"Announce Club Plan at Balboa: Improvement of Property to Follow Reorganization of Project." *Los Angeles Times*, October 24, 1926, E-4.

"Annual Picnic of Minnesotans: State Society Disports over Sands and Waves of Seal Beach." *Los Angeles Times*, July 26, 1914, p.I-9.

"Annual West Coast Surfboard Contest Drawing Many Entries." *Los Angeles Times*, July 4, 1938, p.A-3.

"Aquaplane Is to Be Made Popular." *Los Angeles Times*, January 28, 1919, p.I-5.

"Balboa." *Los Angeles Times*, December 22, 1907, p.II-8.

"Balboa Beach Jazz No Crime. Dance Hall Man Freed by Jury." *Press-Telegram*, September 1, 1927, p.8.

"Balboa to Hold Sport Carnival for Four Days." *Los Angeles Times*, August 1, 1916, p.III-1.

Ball, John "Doc." *California Surfriders, 1946*. Los Angeles: Mountain and Sea Books, 1979.

"Beach Tract Put on Mart." *Los Angeles Times*, July 25, 1926, E-2.

Blake, Tom. *Hawaiian Surfriders, 1935*. Los Angeles: Mountain and Sea Books, 2006.

Boston Publishing Co. *Above and Beyond: A History of the Medal of Honor from the Civil War to Vietnam*. Boston: Boston Publishing Co., 1985.

Brennan, Joseph L. *Duke: The Life Story of Hawaii's Duke Kahanamoku*. Honolulu: Ku Pa'a Publishing, 1994.

Brown, Ralph F. "Natural Landlocked Newport Harbor Seen as Big Future Asset." *Press-Telegram*, October 31, 1925, p.13.

Burdette, Robert J. "Wallowing in the Water." *Los Angeles Times*, February 26, 1910, p.II-4.

"Canoe Sport Is Popular: Balboa Clubmen Propose to Enlarge Fleet." *Los Angeles Times*, April 11, 1909, p.VI-5.

"Capt. Sheffield Resigns Sparr Pavilion Post." *Balboa Times*, May 22, 1930, p.1.

"City Adds to Beaches." *Los Angeles Times*, April 8, 1936, p.A-19.

"Cliff Tucker Upset Winner in San Onofre Surfing Meet." *Los Angeles Times*, August 12, 1940, p.A-10.

"Dead Man at Rum Hearing: Asserted Liquor Runner, Reported Killed in Capture of Yacht, Held to Grand Jury." *Los Angeles Times*, February 28, 1925, p.A-9.

"Dredging at Newport Beach." *Los Angeles Times*, January 9, 1919, p.I-6.

"Duke Kahanamoku Shakes Dust of Hawaii from His Feet and Makes Los Angeles His Home." *Daily Telegram*, September 3, 1922, p.B-1.

"Fearing Flood Call for Bonds: Engineer Reports on Newbert Protection District." *Los Angeles Times*, July 27, 1907, p.II-7.

Felton, James P., ed. *Newport Beach: The First Century, 1888–1988*. Brea, CA: Sultana Press, 1988.

"A Few Things That Newport Can Crow Over." *Los Angeles Times*, August 3, 1883, p.2.

Finney, Ben. *Surfing: A History of the Ancient Hawaiian Sport*. San Francisco: Pomegranate Artbooks, 1996.

"First Rock Is Put in Jetty." *Los Angeles Times*, September 11, 1917, p.I-5.

"Five Are Drowned When Waves Capsize Yacht: Twelve More Narrowly Escape as Swimmer Brings Victims to Shore on Surfboard." *Los Angeles Times*, July 25, 1925, p.A-1.

"G.A. Rogers Succumbs: Dies Aboard His Yacht." *Los Angeles Times*, July 27, 1936, p.A-1.

Gardner, Robert. *Bawdy Balboa*. Brea, CA: Sultana Press, 1992.

"George Freeth, Great Swimmer, Dies Suddenly." *San Diego Union Tribune*, April 8, 1919, p.5.

Gould, Stephen. *Orange County Illustrated: Orange County Before It Was a County*. Hollywood, CA: Sun Dance Press, 1944.

Greenwell, Captain William. Report of the Superintendent, U.S. Coast Survey, 1861. Washington, D.C.: U.S. Government Printing Office, 1861.

"Groynes Advocated to Protect Ocean at Newport Beach." *Press-Telegram*, September 1, 1930, p.B-2.

Hall, Sandra Kimberley. *Memories of Duke: The Legend Comes to Life*. Honolulu: Bess Press, 1995.

"Hawaiian Duke Says Best Surf Riding Is South Newport Harbor Breakwater." *Balboa Times*, August 18, 1922, p.1.

Hoffman, Jeane. "Surfing An Exciting Sport to Ex-gridder, Bob Silver." *Los Angeles Times*, January 27, 1956, p.C-2.

"Holidays Contest to Bar 'Surf Bums.'" *Los Angeles Times*, May 21, 1961, p.CS-4.

"How to Ride a Surfboard: Inside Dope on Managing the Unruly Things." *Los Angeles Times*, June 11, 1922, p.II-14.

Howard, Angus. "Aquaplaning Has Thrills." *Los Angeles Times*, July 22, 1919, p.III-1.

———. "Surf-board Riding Is Some Sport." *Los Angeles Times*, July 13, 1919, p.VI-1.

———. "Surf Canoeing Gives Thrills, Spills." *Los Angeles Times*, July 15, 1919, p.III-1.

"January 1 Dip in Surf Taken As Usual by Swimmer." *Los Angeles Times*, January 2, 1952, p.C-1.

"Jetty Work Completed." *Los Angeles Times*, November 11, 1935, p.10.

"John Lugo First in Sea Horse Beach Contest." *Balboa Times*, July 11, 1929, p.1

"John Lugo Praised for Rescue Work." *Newport Balboa News Times*, October 3, 1939, p.1.

"Kahanamoku Is After Records: George Freeth Is Coaching the Champ." *Los Angeles Times*, July 24, 1914, p.III-2.

Lawrence, Edward C. "Sloop Laurels to Gulf Entry: New Orleans Skipper Takes International Title." *Los Angeles Times*, September 7, 1928, p.B-1.

Lee, Ellen K. *Newport Bay: A Pioneer History*. Fullerton, CA: Sultana Press, 1973.

"Lido Isle To Open Today with Formal Ceremony At Beach: Races, Sport Shows and Music Will be Featured Among Events." *Press-Telegram*, July 8, 1928, p.C-1.

London, Jack. *Learning Hawaiian Surfing: A Royal Sport at Waikiki Beach, Honolulu*. Honolulu: Boom Enterprises, 1983.

"Los Angeles Yacht Club History." July 13, 2012. http://ez-host.org/graphics/uploadfile/4840/5161/la_yacht-club_roster_-history_section_

Maxwell, Evan. "Lessons in Survival from Disastrous 1939 Hurricane." *Los Angeles Times*, September 12, 1971, p.OC-1.

Meyer, Samuel A. *Fifty Golden Years: A History of the City of Newport Beach, 1906–1956*. Newport Beach, CA: Newport Harbor Publishing Co., 1957.

"Miles of Beach Changes Hands. Corona del Mar Traded for Land and Cash." *Los Angeles Times*, February 21, 1915, p.V-1.

"Modjeski Grandson Dies in Beach Home." *Los Angeles Times*, March 30, 1940, p.6.

Nathan, Albert F. "What's Become of the Rum-runners?" *Los Angeles Times*, September 16, 1934, p.H-8.

"New Naval Defense Zone Established in Harbor Area." *Los Angeles Times*, December 20, 1941, p.6.

"Newport: A Small Sized Cyclone Makes Its Appearance." *Los Angeles Times*, March 16, 1882, p.2.

"Newport Bay Site of Attractive Bathing House." *Los Angeles Times*, July 27, 1924, p.D-2.

"Newport Beach Cannery Will Open Soon: Operations at Packing Plant Scheduled to Begin About September 1. *Press-Telegram*, August 27, 1930, p.A-8.

"Newport Beach Scene of Title Surf Clashes." *Los Angeles Times*, September 23, 1932, p.A-11.

"Newport Jetties Started." *Los Angeles Times*, July 10, 1927, p.E-1.

"Newport Plans Aquatic Event." *Los Angeles Times*, September 14, 1934, p.A-15.

"Newport Pleasure Harbor Construction Launches." *Los Angeles Times*, September 23, 1934, p.22.

"Newport Puts Limits on Surfing." *Los Angeles Times*, July 8, 1960, p.C-9.

"Newport Votes Against Name Change: Proposed Shift to Balboa Loses by 1014 to 581." *Press-Telegram*, October 23, 1940, p.B-4.

"Newport's Bonds Win: Great Pleasure Harbor Voted; Orange County Gives 2 to 1 Majority to $640,000 Issue for Project; Government Will Provide $1,195,000 Additional; Jobs for 250 Men." *Los Angeles Times*, December 20, 1933, p.1.

"Newport's Surfing Fee Wiped Out." *Los Angeles Times*, December 17, 1969, p.D-9.

"Novel Surfboard and Canoes Made." *Long Beach Press*, February 26, 1921, B-1.

"Olympic Girl Swimmer from Canada Wins Sunday Contest." *Costa Mesa Herald*, September 29, 1932, p.9.

"Orange County Beaches." *Los Angeles Times*, January 1, 1898, p.39.

"Orange County Building Wonderful Coast Road." *Los Angeles Times*, February 7, 1915, p.VII-3.

Orange County Historical Society. *Orange County: Postcard History Series*. Charleston, SC: Arcadia Publishing, 2005.

"Orange Co. Lively Fourth at Balboa." *Los Angeles Times*, July 1, 1913, p.II-7.

"Orphans Flee as River Alters Map of County." *Los Angeles Times*, January 22, 1916, p.II-1.

"Palisades Clubhouse Is Planned." *Los Angeles Times*, June 14, 1925.

"Peterson and Harrison Loom as Favorites in Surfing Tourney." *Los Angeles Times*, July 13, 1940, p.12.

"Peterson Wins Surf Contest." *Los Angeles Times*, September 26, 1932, p.A-11.

"Preston Peterson Captures Watermen's All-around Title." *Los Angeles Times*, November 12, 1941, p.19.

"Riding Breakers Great Sport with Auto Shoes." *Los Angeles Times*, July 25, 1915, p.VI-8.

"Riding Surfboard Thrills. George Freeth Is Teaching Girls at Redondo." *Los Angeles Times*, July 14, 1912, p.VII-10.

Robbins, Gary. "O.C.'s Great Flood of 1938." *Orange County Register*, March 3, 1998, p.A-1.

Ruhlow, Jerry. "Lifeguards Rescue Man Swept to Sea in an Inner Tube." *Los Angeles Times*, January 27, 1969, p.C1.

"Sand Flows from Pumps." *Los Angeles Times*, January 10, 1935, p.A-5.

"Santa Ana Election: Citizens Vote to Organize Newbert Protection District." *Los Angeles Times*, May 23, 1907, p.II-13.

"Santa Ana River's Raging Flood Takes Heavy Toll in Three Counties." *Los Angeles Times*, March 4, 1938, p.5

"Seaside Cities Prepare to Celebrate as New State Coastline Highway Nears Completion." *Los Angeles Times*, March 15, 1925, p.H-1.

Seward, E.D. "Duke Entertains Balboa with Surfboard Stunts." *Los Angeles Times*, September 15, 1914, p.III-4.

Shanahan, Dennis. *Old Redondo: A Pictorial History of Redondo Beach, California.* Redondo Beach, CA: Legends Press, 1982.

Sherman, Henry Lancey. *A History of Newport Beach.* Newport Beach, CA: City of Newport Beach, 1931.

"Shifting River Mouth Leaves Knotty Problem." *Los Angeles Times*, May 18, 1916, p.I-5.

Smith, Mark Chalon. "A 'Beach Boy' Remains Immersed in His Craft Canoeing." Los Angeles Times, September 9, 1993, p.1.

Bibliography

"Solo Surfing Loses Out in Hermosa Fete." *Los Angeles Times*, July 2, 1961, p.CS-8.

"Southland Starts Rebuilding; Storm Death Toll Now Eighty-five; Fate of 130 in Doubt as Skies Clear." *Los Angeles Times*, March 5, 1938, p.1.

"Spills Mark Surf Contest at San Onofre." *Los Angeles Times*, July 11, 1938, p.A-9.

"Stose Brings Back the Bacon: Winner of Race to Hawaii Returns." *Los Angeles Times*, July 1, 1928, p.A-2.

"Surf and Paddleboard Riders Win Awards in First Tourney." *Los Angeles Times*, August 28, 1939, p.18.

"Surfboard Club Works." *Press-Telegram*, May 17, 1931, p.B-1.

"Surf Club Is Formed to Ride the Waves." *Los Angeles Times*, November 8, 1912, p.III-4.

"Surf Riders." *Los Angeles Times*, April 14, 1940, p.H-3.

"Surf Sled Tames Wild Waves: New Board Will Ride Roughest Swells." *Los Angeles Times*, May 19, 1932, p.A-10.

"Surfing Novelty: Pillow Case Riding New Sport." *Press-Telegram*, August 6, 1939, p.B-1.

Thorpe, James. *Henry Edwards Huntington: A Biography*. Los Angeles: University of California Press, 1994.

"Thousands Witness Surf Battle to Save Pair at Huntington Beach Pier." *Los Angeles Times*, July 29, 1935, p.14.

"Twelve Saved from Sea by Rescuers: Duke Kahanamoku, Famous Hawaiian Swimmer, Hero of Tragedy." *Press-Telegram*, June 15, 1925, p.A-5.

U.S. Senate Committee on Veterans' Affairs. *Medal of Honor Recipients, 1863–1978*. Washington, D.C.: Government Printing Office, 1979.

Vultee, John. "History of Newport, Balboa, Corona del Mar Surfing." Unpublished. Part of John Vultee Collection, Surfing Heritage Foundation.

"War Craft Enters Harbor; Proves Advantages of New Jetty." *Los Angeles Times*, May 11, 1919, p.I-11.

"Water Pageant at Balboa. Canoe Tilting Match." *Los Angeles Times*, August 25, 1908, p.II-9.

Bibliography

Waterman. "Waikiki Beachboy George Freeth Becomes the First Lifeguard in Southern California, 1883–1919." http://www.surfart.com/lifegd3.htm (7 June 1998).

Westfall, Douglas. *The History of Corona del Mar*. Orange, CA: Paragon, 2004.

Wiegel, Robert. *San Pedro Bay Delta, in Southern California Shore and Shore Use Changes During Past 1 ½ Centuries from a Coastal Engineering Perspective*. Berkeley, University of California Water Resources Center, 2009.

Young, Betty Lou. *Our First Century: The Los Angeles Athletic Club, 1880–1980*. Los Angeles, LAAC Press, 1979.

Young, Nat. *The History of Surfing*. Palm Beach, New South Whales: Palm Beach Press, 1987.

Index

U

V

W

Y